WHAT YOUR CHILD ON THE SPECTRUM REALLY NEEDS

Advice from 12 Autistic Adults

JENNA GENSIC

PO Box 861116
Shawnee, KS 66286
www.aapcpublishing.com

Publisher's Cataloging-In-Publication

Names: Gensic, Jenna, author.
Title: What your child on the spectrum really needs : advice from 12 autistic adults / Jenna Gensic.
Description: Shawnee, KS : AAPC Publishing, [2020]
Identifiers: ISBN: 9781942197539 (pbk.) | 9781942197546 (ebook)
Subjects: LCSH: Parents of autistic children--Handbooks, manuals, etc. | Parents of children with disabilities--Handbooks, manuals, etc. | Children with autism spectrum disorders--Handbooks, manuals, etc. | Children with autism spectrum disorders--Family relationships. | Autism spectrum disorders in children--Treatment. | Asperger's syndrome in children--Treatment. | Autism in children--Treatment. | Sensory integration dysfunction in children--Treatment. | Social skills in children--Study and teaching. | Language disorders in children--Treatment. | Autistic children--Education. | Children with autism spectrum disorders--Education. | Asperger's syndrome--Patients--Education.
Classification: LCC: RJ506.A9 G46 2020 | DDC: 618.92/858832--dc23

Table of Contents

Chapter Eight:

Friendship and Sexuality Throughout Adolescence - An Interview With Amy Gravino

Chapter Nine:

Redefining Communication - An Interview With Brian King

Chapter Ten:

The Empathy Myth and Educational Advocacy - An Interview With Shawna Hinkle

Chapter Eleven:

Succeeding in the Workplace - An Interview With Gavin Bollard

Introduction

I believe people tell stories to make sense of their lives and to help others. When my oldest son was born three months prematurely in 2008 and spent six months in the hospital, I began reading and writing essays about the neonatal intensive care unit experience to make sense of my unexpected situation.

I am a planner. My husband and I thought we had timed our pregnancy perfectly. My due date was late May and, since we were both teachers, we planned to use our summer off from work to begin learning to become parents. I had followed the dietary guidelines and adhered to the recommended exercise restrictions to ensure the best possible beginning for our baby, but our son's early birth and the host of medical complications that followed led to the shocking realization that I couldn't control every aspect of my life.

As my son grew older and was diagnosed with cerebral palsy and autism, I became interested in connecting with other families who had children with disabilities, and I also immersed myself in the advice of medical and educational specialists in order to understand more about my son's conditions and how my husband and I could help him.

But after a few years of following the professionals, I felt limited in my pursuit of the medical, psychological, and behavioral advice from the experts. Instead, I turned to books and memoirs by parents offering advice based on their experiences raising their autistic children. These books have valuable information and are useful to other parents of children on the spectrum who want to read about someone experiencing similar life obstacles and triumphs.

As time went on, I also began following the work of autistic self-advocates in an effort to learn even more about the path my son was on. In particular, I was interested in finding out what individuals on the spectrum felt about the different treatment approaches their parents had taken over the years. I knew there were organizations (led by parents, doctors, scientists, and researchers) whose mission was to help parents sort out the fact from the fluff within the barrage of treatments, therapies, medications, and diet advice, but I wanted to know how autistic individuals felt about these ideas. So I interviewed autistic adults and learned what parents, friends, or teachers had done for (or to) them that helped and hurt them – whether intentionally or not. This is where I should have started.

When I began the interviews, I expected to learn about the effectiveness of certain therapies or treatments; however, I was surprised to discover the range of advice the contributors offered, including many ways families can better understand their children's neurology, support language and behavior development, and demonstrate love and respect for their autistic members. Through this process, I gained a refreshing perspective that has changed the way I talk about autism and select and implement therapies and supports for my son.

This book is a result of some of those interviews. I trust other parents can benefit from this knowledge as well.

Embracing Autism

I've learned to become more aware of the language I use to talk about autism and how the words I use communicate how I value my son. I vigilantly aim to use language that communicates my unconditional love and confidence in his human worth. I think it's important for parents to discuss the language they will use to talk about their child and practice that language from a very young age. Children are perceptive and part of their self-concept can be based on the language you use about them and their autism. This book offers useful tips for speaking about autism in a way that will help your child thrive and grow up to be an independent self-advocate.

My son's autism diagnosis didn't come as a shock to us, but he had recently been diagnosed with cerebral palsy, and we were rattled by a new neurological condition to explore and support. His speech therapist at the time helped us put his diagnosis in perspective. She said, "He's still your son. The label hasn't changed that. He's still the same kid." She was right. This sounds like pretty basic advice, but it is an important principle to accepting and benefiting from many of the recommendations in this book. Nothing grabbed my son hostage when he turned 4. Rather, a psychologist explained his neurology a little better to us so we could help support him throughout his life.

I've learned to embrace my son's autism as an asset to his development. I don't have personal or professional experience with nonverbal children or adults. But I know that for my son, his autistic identity has had some powerful beneficial effects at this point in his life, including the following:

▶▶ His early reading and writing skills have allowed him to gain confidence as a peer tutor to other children in his class as well as to his younger siblings.

▶▶ His early fascination with writing and drawing has led to a special interest in creating fiction and nonfiction chapter books. This intense writing practice has also helped him develop incredible handwriting skills and overcome some of the fine-motor issues he had due to his cerebral palsy. He writes much better than most nondisabled students much older than him!

▶▶ His academic interests have given him a social edge. His classmates view him as smart (although we prefer the term *hard worker*) and capable. Because of his delayed gross-motor skills, at times, it is hard for him to keep up with the fast physical play of his peers. His study of a wide range of subjects enables him to speak intelligently about them and is therefore able to contribute something valuable to his peers each day.

I believe it is crucial not to isolate autistic individuals but to cultivate their skills. Grandin and Panek (2014) asserted, "If you really want to prepare kids to participate in the mainstream of life, then you have to do more than accommodate their deficits. You have to figure out ways to exploit their strengths" (p. 184). We should support autistic individuals like we support neurotypicals (NTs), addressing their deficits and encouraging their strengths. We should value some of the autistic-like tendencies (e.g., an exceptional ability to memorize material or to talk at length about any topic they are fascinated with); help autistic individuals learn when, where, and how to use their strengths; and not dismiss them as quirky or weird.

Advocacy

I am a strong supporter of the concept of neurodiversity. In *Neurotribes* (2015), Steve Silberman explains that neurodiversity advocates believe autism is not a problem with nature or a puzzle that needs to be solved or eliminated by selective abortion. Instead, he proposes that "Society should regard it [autism] as a valuable part of humanity's genetic legacy while ameliorating the aspects of autism that can be profoundly disabling without adequate forms of support" (pp. 464-465).

The neurodiversity viewpoint is rooted in the desire for equal rights and treatment in society. Most neurodiversity advocates support research into the causes of autism and ways to lessen some of the disabling symptoms. No one person can speak for all people on the spectrum. It's important to continually gather research and never stop engaging with autistic people themselves.

Lydia Brown wrote a blog post about advocacy inspired by her friend and fellow disability rights activist, Ki'tay Davidson, who passed away suddenly in 2014. Davidson was a regular spokesperson for change and spoke about the duty of being an advocate. Indeed, he was honored at the White House with Lydia in 2013 as one of the "Champions of Change" for disability rights on the anniversary of the Americans With Disabilities Act of 1999. During a panel discussion, Davidson said,

> Advocacy is not just a task for charismatic individuals or high profile community organizers. Advocacy is for all of us; advocacy is a way of life. It is a natural response to the injustices and inequality in the world. While you and I may not have the sole responsibility for these inequities, that does not alter its reality. **(Brown, 2014, para. 21)**

Parents of autistic children can provide a secondary, yet powerful and worthy voice in the conversation for the rights of individuals on the spectrum. Autistic people can benefit from the help of advocates who want to assist them in obtaining crucial academic, social, emotional, and career support services, but they first need advocates to validate who they are as humans and promote their intrinsic value.

I wanted the approach of this book to also underscore the main message: ***People on the spectrum are valuable and should lead the public conversation about autism.*** As such, this is a book about the authority of human experience. There is much to gain by listening to people talk about their experiences. I have learned much from these contributors that I could never have grasped from reading a medical journal; consulting with any of my son's doctors and educators; or talking to other parents of autistic children. This book is my effort to support autistics whose voices are not acknowledged enough in the neurotypical world. I hope this book helps change the way you think about autism and your children. Writing it has done so for me.

How The Chapters Are Organized

The chapters in the book profile 12 autistic adults with diverse backgrounds, jobs, and accomplishments. In my efforts to find people to interview, I began by searching online for people active in the autistic community either in their published writings, blogs, or public speaking. I was also contacted by two adult autistics after they heard about the project I was working on.

When selecting contributors, I chose to focus on the stories of people who were verbal, interested in autism self-advocacy, and represented a variety of educational and professional backgrounds. I conducted the interviews via Skype and email over a three-year period. Some of the contributors have public platforms speaking about autism awareness and acceptance, and all of them are interested in telling their stories in order to help other families and their children on the spectrum.

All of them are autistic, and half of them have autistic children. Some have differing views regarding autism, but they all have valuable advice for parents of autistic children and young adults. Each chapter reveals personal stories and real-life examples of obstacles and personal struggles the contributor faced growing up autistic, followed by reflection questions, tips for parents, and resources.

Language

The use of person-first language and identity-first language is discussed both in Chapter One by Lydia Brown and in the Appendix. In this book, I describe individuals on the spectrum using identity-first language because this represents the preference of the autistic individuals I've interviewed. If a contributor has chosen verbiage to use, I have attempted to honor that preference. In addition, the use of the male pronoun is generally used except (a) when talking about issues that specifically are related by women or related to women and (b) when contributors have requested that gender-neutral pronouns be used.

Scope

The contributors in each chapter speak about their experience growing up with autism spectrum disorder (ASD). If you were to further categorize them, you might say the majority are high-functioning autistics (HFAs). However, I resist using this term because it is sometimes limiting and misleading. Besides, many of the contributors take offense to attempts to categorize specific autism symptoms. I have not included individuals with severe communication disabilities in an effort to learn more about adults on the spectrum with skills that matched those of my son. Despite this distinctive focus, much of the advice in this book is applicable to individuals anywhere on the spectrum.

THIS BOOK IS NOT:

▸▸ A representation of all individuals on the spectrum. Rather, the stories are a representation of the individual experiences of the contributors as autistic humans.

▸▸ A collection of case studies. I have cited some case studies as they relate to or support the advice given by an autistic contributor.

▸▸ A work that speculates about the causes of autism and ways to prevent it.

▸▸ Organized medical advice from experts. Again, supporting research is cited when applicable in order to augment recommendations the contributors have made.

THIS BOOK IS:

▸▸ Respectful of the voice of the autistic individual.

▸▸ Full of stories, opinions, and tips.

▸▸ Based on the personal experiences of adult verbal autistics.

▸▸ Relevant for parents and caregivers of young autistic children, adolescents, and adults.

▸▸ Focused on acceptance and how to offer appropriate supports to improve the lives of autistic people now.

▸▸ Easy-to-understand and immediately applicable for parents interested in autism advocacy.

Chapter One

The Problem With "Fixing" Your Child

AN INTERVIEW WITH LYDIA BROWN

> *Autistics are not defective neurotypicals. We're perfectly happy, perfectly functioning autistics.*
>
> LYDIA BROWN

EXPOSING UNCONSCIOUS PATRONIZATION

Lydia Brown[1], a national public speaker and autism advocate, scanned the posters around the room at the National Transition Conference, organized to help students with disabilities transition to adulthood, adult services, postsecondary education, or the workforce. Already beginning to establish a national platform as a disability rights activist, Lydia was attending the conference as the Patricia Morrisey Disability Policy Fellow at the Institute for Educational Leadership. On that day, one particular poster caught Lydia's attention. The presenter discussed her research related to autism and transitions to adolescence. After listening for a while, Lydia attempted to join the conversation.

"Well, I'm an autistic person," Lydia began, but was immediately interrupted.

"You mean you are a person who has autism," another conference attendee corrected. But these perhaps well-intentioned words fell on the deaf ears of an educated, self-aware, and passionate autistic rights advocate who wouldn't sit idly by while patronized by another person.

"Actually, I call myself an autistic person intentionally and have written three published essays about person-first language," Lydia responded.

[1]*Lydia prefers to be identified using gender-neutral pronouns.*

At this time, the presenter chimed in to support Lydia by offering a brief explanation of how some disability communities disagree with the universal push to use person-first language because of its attempt to separate the disability from personhood, presuming the disability isn't tied to a person's identity and suggesting it is something awful that people would want to cast off or be separated from.

Lydia appreciated finding an NT special education teacher who was knowledgeable about the opposition to person-first language. Lydia's willingness to speak up in this situation helps expose the perceived power differential some nondisabled individuals have towards the disabled community.

Lydia prefers identify-first language and opposes the practice of coaching people to use person-first language:

> You shouldn't be correcting disabled people with how they want to be identified. But because of the power differential, disabled people are viewed as not capable of making these decisions for themselves. You shouldn't have to assert that you are a person if you are disabled. It shouldn't detract from all the other parts of your identity. Autism isn't the only part of my identity, but it is a part of it. It is a significant, informative and foundational part of my identity.

But this preference isn't universal among all people on the spectrum. Lydia recommends determining someone's identity preference when possible and not assuming your personal preference is the most appropriate way to refer to everyone on the spectrum.

THE PROBLEM WITH AN AUTISM LABEL

Lydia prefers not to categorize someone's autism and chooses not to reveal the specificity of her own diagnosis. Labels such as high- and low-functioning, for example, and even the pre-DSM-5 (American Psychiatric Association, 2000) labels of Asperger Syndrome or Pervasive Developmental Disorder - Not Otherwise Specified can inaccurately and unfairly cast judgment on a person on the spectrum. Lydia believes people use diagnostic labels to categorize people and justify stereotypes, creating artificial dividing lines between high and low functioning and many other labels. Although "high-functioning autism" is not an official diagnostic label, the mainstream public often uses this term to describe individuals on the spectrum with average or above average intelligences (Williams & Roberts, 2015, p. 216). Lydia explains that most people use this term to mean that autistic people can exhibit behaviors that make them appear to function similar to other NTs in the mainstream environment.

"So in the autistic community with a capital A, it seems that the very strong preference is to refer to ourselves as autistic people, not people with autism. Now that's a very intentional thing."

So what's wrong the term high functioning? Lydia believes a label of high functioning isn't as descriptive as many people think it is. Some autistic people are high functioning when it comes to one skill (in other words, they can perform it well by the standards of a mainstream society), but low functioning when asked to perform a different task (or the same task in a different setting). This is true of everyone whether or not they are on the spectrum. Similarly, autistic people who are identified as low functioning may have high-functioning skills as well. Thus, these terms suggest a false sense of identification and don't do justice to the unique skill sets of people all over the spectrum.

Another problem with separating autistic people into discrete categories is that such generalized categories impact society's expectations of each group. Lydia says some people believe "Aspies" are the next step up on the evolutionary ladder whereas those with more severe forms of autism are "broken." Some people assume high-functioning autism isn't really disabling and even that the label comes with the advantage of possessing a special talent or superior intelligence. Tim Page (see Chapter Four) agrees:

> There has become this romanticization of Asperger's syndrome where mothers who would be horrified if they were told their child was autistic are okay with them being told they have Asperger's because this means that they're little geniuses, brilliant, charming ... and that really refers to just a small set of people. Also, autistic people are so often treated as if they are human rubbish; they are thrown into the trash can, and no one thinks they can be reclaimed, and I don't think that's true either, so I like the idea of a spectrum.

Jim Sinclair, an autistic writer, speaker, and disability rights advocate, discusses his experience with the assumptions of those around him in his personal essay "Bridging the Gaps: An Inside-Out View of Autism (Or, Do You Know What I Don't Know?)" (1992). Jim explains what he believes are the most damaging and painful assumptions: "... that I understand what is expected of me, that I know how to do it, and that I fail to perform as expected out of deliberate spite or unconscious hostility" (Schopler & Mesibov, 2013, p. 296).

Lydia says people think they are offering compliments by attempting to categorize autism with statements like, "You must be high-functioning." But these people misunderstand autism and can patronize those on the spectrum.

Ben Kartje (see Chapter Three), agrees,

> When a doctor or another person refers to me as being on the "high-functioning" end of the spectrum, that doesn't really make sense to me. Does that mean that I'm almost "normal"? What pops into my head is, "There's Ben; he's that dot right there!" Like they're graphing the whole thing. I don't really understand what they are basing their decision on. What is normal? Do people think it is a compliment to be considered "high functioning"? To be considered "almost normal"?

Autism Labels and Parent/Caregiver Assumptions

The assumptions that come along with functionality labels fail to acknowledge the individual's full neurological condition, which still results in a multitude of obstacles to daily functioning. Psychologist Barry M. Prizant, Ph.D., has seen this in his work with autistic children. In Uniquely Human (Prizant & Fields-Meyer, 2015), he writes, "Even when a child is described as 'high-functioning,' parents often point out that he continues to experience major challenges that educators and others too often minimize or ignore" (p. 221). A label of low-functioning might mean people have low expectations, whereas a label of high-functioning could give the false notion that everything is fine.

STOP TRYING TO "FIX" US

Some autistic people want society to deemphasize what is negative about autism. While Lydia and many others admit their autism is a disability, Lydia only describes it as such because of how our culture and environment favors NTs. In other words, having a disability is neutral, not negative; this is often articulated as the social model of disability. The medical model of disability, on the other hand, identifies disability as an abnormality and a clear disadvantage that should be cured or eradicated. Adherents of the medical model support accommodations for disabled persons, including those on the spectrum.

Many autistic people prefer not to be changed or cured, but rather to live in an environment that is accepting of neurodiversity. That is, they would like to live as their autistic selves without the pressures to conform to NT expectations of different social behaviors. In Lydia's words, "I do not have challenges because I am autistic. What makes life difficult is when people do not accommodate for them."

> **Jim Sinclair has written extensively on this topic, including the following:**
> Autism isn't something a person has, or a 'shell' that a person is trapped inside. There's no normal child hidden behind the autism. Autism is a way of being. It is pervasive; it colors every experience, every sensation, perception, thought, emotion, and encounter, every aspect of existence. It is not possible to separate the autism from the person – and if it were possible, the person you'd have left would not be the same person you started with ... Therefore, when parents say, "I wish my child did not have autism," what they're really saying is, "I wish the autistic child that I have did not exist and I had a different (non-autistic child) instead." This is what we hear when you mourn over our existence. This is what we hear when you pray for a cure. This is what we know, when you tell us of your fondest hopes and dreams for us; that your greatest wish is that one day we will cease to be, and strangers you can love will move in behind our faces. (Sinclair, 1993)

According to Lydia and many others, the problem with many therapies, however well meant, is that they tend to use a top-down approach of eliminating harmless social quirks, perpetuating the belief that some idea of NT communication is morally superior and the autistic way is shameful or embarrassing. Penni Winter (2012), like Lydia, an autistic writer from New Zealand, articulates this distinction:

> The normalization approach can involve many different therapies and practices. Let me make it clear – it's not what's done, but why it's done. Some of the same therapies, such as social skills and life skills training, I know are used by those who

don't subscribe to the Big Bad Autism viewpoint. They are seeking instead to simply grow their child's capabilities as an autistic person, an approach I have started calling 'Maximization,' and a goal I wholeheartedly support. With normalization, on the other hand, the ultimate goal is simply to rid the individual of any outward sign of their Autism. (pp. 115-116)

This does not mean that parents should stop searching for ways to help their autistic children. Rather, it is a suggestion that parents rethink why they are trying to help them. If parents' expectations are that their children need to be fixed, they may frustrate and hurt their autistic children. However, if they are able to find a way to be sensitive to their children's needs and interests, they can help them seek therapy options related to specific goals. Therapy or support groups can be effective for individuals on the spectrum if, as Lydia puts it, they "affirm or respect the autistic people there and are centered around coping mechanisms, support systems, self-accommodation, and self-advocacy."

SELF-ADVOCACY

Lydia encourages self-advocacy for everyone on the spectrum and works to make policy changes that support autistic people. She believes some autistic people may find peace and freedom through self-advocacy channels and finding others who share their interests or struggles. It is the work of autism advocates and self-advocates that has progressed the disability rights movement, and the more voices heard helps make more changes possible. For more self-advocacy tips, see Chapter Fifteen.

REFLECTION QUESTIONS

▶▶ Do you favor the medical or social model of disability?

▶▶ Which style of language do you prefer, person-first or identify-first? Which style does your child prefer? What are the reasons for the type of language you choose?

▶▶ Do you find yourself talking about ideas for "treating" your child's autism or hoping eventually your child will be "cured"? How does your child feel about this language? Does your child want to be cured?

▶▶ How can autism awareness or autism acceptance be promoted within your family or community?

Chapter Two

Social Integration And
The Problem With Hiding Autism
AN INTERVIEW WITH ALYSSA HILLARY

It's not that people are more accepting. I have more power to choose who I will interact with, and if you're not accepting, I'm not going to deal with you.

ALYSSA HILLARY

SARCASM AND JOKES

Twenty-three-year-old Alyssa Hillary[2] almost always struggles to read people, and due to this challenge, Alyssa's conversations often take confusing turns. For example, when talking to somebody, sometimes Alyssa realizes a few minutes later that rather than being literal, the other person was joking or being sarcastic. At other times, it may take years for her to make this connection. In either case, the flow of communication is interrupted, causing frustration, confusion, and an awkward disconnect. Alyssa experiences this on a regular basis as illustrated in the following examples:

▶▶ On the first day of a college class, Alyssa walked into a classroom and asked, "Is this econ?" The teacher responded, "No, philosophy," so Alyssa left. A student in the class got up to call Alyssa back in and say that it was, in fact, the econ classroom and that the professor was only joking. Alyssa was the brunt of the professor's humor throughout the class.

▶▶ In fifth and sixth grade, Alyssa reported to a teacher (on several occasions) when a peer said she was going to kill herself. The peer was upset with Alyssa for taking her

[2] *Alyssa prefers to be identified using gender-neutral pronouns.*

seriously and telling an adult since she claimed she was only joking. Alyssa said the peer wasn't being honest, it wasn't just a joke – it was a call for attention. This was hard for Alyssa to decipher and certainly not something to lightly dismiss. Alyssa explains that sometimes it is difficult to interpret what people truly think or feel because of the many different ways people convey meaning.

▸▸ One day in high school when Alyssa and a friend were walking down the hall, a friend pointed out a piece of equipment on the hallway ceiling and joked that it was a signal scrambler to prevent students from using their cell phones in school. Alyssa assumed the friend was serious at the time and only realized several years later that the friend was joking.

Alyssa readily admits that autistic people can benefit from identifying and understanding sarcasm, figurative language, and jokes; however, at the same time, she points out that society's expectations for communication are too often one-sided, favoring the NT standards and requiring everyone else to match them. "Telling someone that the only way they know how to communicate is wrong and only speaking to them in ways that they cognitively can't understand is not making the world accessible for people with disabilities, and accessibility is important," Alyssa says.

Alyssa challenges others to be sensitive to those who tend to view language more literally than they do. For example, when asked if they're being sarcastic, or if they're joking, they should answer honestly and explain their metaphors, and, in general, they should try to avoid using that kind of language in the presence of their autistic peers.

WHAT IS SOCIAL INTEGRATION?

As mentioned, Alyssa found it hard to integrate with peers because of the prevailing use of sarcasm and joking. Another difficulty with regard to social integration stems from society's general discouragement of stimming (self-stimulating behavior). Many autistic people are trained to have "quiet hands" (no hand flapping or fidgeting) or to refrain from other adaptive behaviors, such as rocking, because such behaviors may be seen as awkward or unusual. By discouraging stimming, the behaviors are removed from the public eye, perpetuating the idea that autistics cannot be socially integrated unless natural behaviors are stifled.

In his article "What Is 'Stimming' and Why Is It Important?," Gavin Bollard (see Chapter Eleven) notes, "Stimming is normal and we all do it. Perhaps we don't do it to the same extent as people on the autism spectrum, but maybe that's just because we've found other, 'more civilised' ways to stim" (para. 9, 2012). For example, it tends to be more acceptable to bite your nails, tap a pencil, drum your fingers, or bob your leg up and down than to hand flap or rock back and forth.

Alyssa stresses the importance of accepting autistic behaviors like stimming rather than isolating the people who exhibit them. According to Alyssa, autism shouldn't have to disappear in order for someone on the spectrum to be accepted.

"Maybe we're the favorite target, and that means we have more incidents of bullying to deal with. Maybe it's more often. Maybe it's more severe. Maybe the bullies are getting bolder and bolder as our teachers turn a blind eye. Maybe we're taking the bullies at their word when our neurotypical peers can detect what is exaggeration and what needs to be taken seriously. I know that all happened to me."

"Atypical" Behaviors

Atypical behaviors are not necessarily immoral or intolerable; they just differ from the norm. Prizant and Fields-Meyer (2015) explain that we should not view them simply as behaviors – "They are most often strategies to cope with dysregulation" (p. 22). Sometimes children on the spectrum behave atypically as a way of emotionally self-regulating in order to function (Prizant & Fields-Meyer, 2015). Children need to know that their existence is accepted and that they will be supported in their individual interests and goals. Maybe fitting in, being the same, or passing as NT shouldn't be the goal, but rather, self-actualization or fulfilling human potential should be the goal. The United Nations Department of Economic and Social Affairs (2005) views social integration as a "dynamic and principled process where all members participate in dialogue to achieve and maintain peaceful social relations. Social integration does not mean coerced assimilation or forced integration." Social integration requires everyone – both on and off the spectrum – to work together to live in mutual respect.

HIDING AUTISM

Many autistics are often implicitly or explicitly told to hide their autism, which causes them to internalize the belief that autism is bad and that the safest thing to do is to hide their autistic behaviors even if it's not supportive of their life goals. According to Alyssa, "I definitely had teachers tell me that I couldn't get away with flapping or rocking 'in the real world.' And I'm a teacher and a writer and a graduate student. I can definitely get away with flapping and rocking." Some individuals on the spectrum may not have a supportive peer group or even family to make them feel comfortable living as autistic people. In these situations, daily life can be physically exhausting.

Alyssa, along with many autistic people, makes regular efforts to fit in with peers and colleagues, but becomes discouraged if they feel they must hide their autism, repeatedly repressing their natural selves. Alyssa explains that sometimes people's "cluelessness" helped make acceptance slightly easier. For example, academically gifted, Alyssa exploited the assumption that "gifted kids are weird" as a social smoke screen. But constant name calling in the third grade caused Alyssa to conceal hand flapping. It took nearly 10 years for Alyssa to feel comfortable flapping. Amy Gravino (see Chapter Eight) realized that hiding her association with autism wasn't accurate or helpful. "I used to be very afraid of being associated with people diagnosed with classic autism. But one day I realized that people with classic autism are going through the same things I am."

Parents and therapists should be aware of the social implications communicated when correcting behaviors. While some behaviors that may harm self or others physically or emotionally need to be addressed and modified for the safety of everyone involved, the same justification doesn't hold for eliminating autistic behaviors, such as hand flapping.

Normalcy should not be the end goal. Instead, parents and caregivers have an obligation to help their autistic children grow to lead happy and meaningful lives while living as a minority within the neurodiversity pool. When children are young, parents must determine what skills they believe are necessary to thrive. But, when possible, autistic individuals should be an integral part of shaping their own life paths and communicating what they want and need in order to achieve their goals.

> "Hiding sucked. One of the few things I ever tried to hide ... was the flapping, since my classmates in third grade kept calling me r******* over it ... I didn't feel safe flapping openly again until about a year ago, though I still did it under certain circumstances because I wasn't always capable of not flapping."

The Effects of Hiding Autism

Cary Terra (2012), a psychotherapist specializing in working with adults on the autism spectrum, discusses on her blog, Aspiestrategy.com, the characteristics of the "hidden autistic" and the unhealthy physical and emotional consequences this behavior might pose. Terra talks about one of her patients whom she described as "quietly confident and wry, intelligent and perceptive." People responded well to him, really liked him. In fact, Terra's colleague even ridiculed his diagnosis of Asperger Syndrome because he seemed to function so well around others. But while her patient appeared comfortable with and capable of carrying out the socialization requirements of a typical day, he was returning home exhausted. Terra writes, "His wife comes home to a man who has retreated to isolation as a desperate attempt to find peace and rest" (para. 8, 2012). Many people who live with someone on the spectrum understand this sort of fatigue. Terra worries that "hidden autistics" carry a tremendously difficult daily burden that may have dangerous long-term mental health consequences for both autistic people and their spouses or children.

REFLECTION QUESTIONS

▶▶ How do you know if your child understands sarcasm?

▶▶ What does social integration look like?

▶▶ What behaviors do you ask your child to change or eliminate?

▶▶ Have you attempted to shed your child's diagnosis, either by repetitive retesting or refusing to tell family or friends of the label? What are your reasons for this?

▶▶ How does your child feel about having a label of autism?

Chapter Three

Establishing A Safe Environment At Home And At School

AN INTERVIEW WITH BEN KARTJE

Autism has made me who I am today.

BEN KARTJE

BY THE BOOK

Ben Kartje was teased for following the rules. He adhered to his private school dress code: always tucked his shirt in and only wore regulation dress pants. He always sat in his assigned seat.

"I was an outcast."

Although this was what the adults in his life expected of him, it was a source of ridicule from his peers. They also enjoyed watching him get angry. They would call him Benjamin Franklin as he worked on his assignments and laugh as they watched him tense up. He would try to ignore them, but his obvious irritation led to more teasing.

"The instance [of bullying] ... has stuck with me most of my life and probably helped form who I am today."

Telling them to stop or going to the teacher never helped; they called him a tattletale and continued pestering him outside the classroom walls and behind the teacher's back. Ben struggled to follow the rules and avoid ridicule, which added to the existing stress of trying to meet his academic expectations.

But not everyone was cruel to Ben. Some of his peers, even a handful of popular ones, were cordial to him when they crossed paths. But their politeness was superficial. Although Ben considered them friends, they never really wanted to include him. They never chose him to be on their teams or invited him to any activities outside of school. "They never saw me as a real friend."

"I was never invited to anything."

In high school, Ben became fed up with constantly worrying about what others thought of him. His parents tried to intervene and even sent him to the local public school for more academic and social supports. But unfortunately, Ben felt the public school had expectations that failed to address his unique learning needs. He was one of many students with an individualized education program (IEP), but his needs were often overlooked as staff attempted to manage others students with more visible needs.

Eventually, he returned to his former private school and sought advice from a guidance counselor about the constant teasing and the difficulty he had with meeting expectations. The counselor encouraged Ben to take off the "mask" he wore every day in order to relieve some of his stress. Ben also visited a priest who gave him similar advice, "Be who God made you to be. Don't be anyone else." Ben heeded this advice and gained confidence once he stopped trying to control what his peers thought of him.

"I kept telling myself don't let anybody tell you who you are. Just be who you were meant to be. Just be yourself. That's the only way you are going to be happy. If you pretend to be someone you are not, you are going to put on a mask. You are not going to like the ending."

CLASSROOM MANAGEMENT

Ben struggled academically, but was determined to finish high school. He gradually gained confidence in his autistic identity and did not care as much about what others thought of him, but the day-to-day social interactions still unnerved him. Ben found it easier to tolerate the demands of school in a well-managed classroom, which he found at the private school he attended. Out-of-control classrooms can stress any student, but autistic students who crave predictability and routine tend to have a more difficult time thriving in these environments. A well-managed environment offers autistic students the best opportunity to learn and successfully meet teacher expectations. When a teacher creates an atmosphere of mutual respect and leads students with clear and firm expectations, everyone in the class benefits. On one hand, unaddressed misbehavior and loosely adhered-to policies open the door for unpredictability and chaos and negatively impact learning potentials. On the other hand, well-managed classrooms provide autistic students a familiar, comfortable place to open their minds to new learning opportunities.

Not all well-managed classrooms look the same, but Ben noted the following indicators of a safe, structured environment:

▸▸ Clearly-defined rules or expectations
▸▸ Clearly-established classroom routines
▸▸ Constantly engaged students with little or no "down time"
▸▸ A tone of mutual respect between the teacher and students

It helped Ben to walk into a classroom where the teacher was prepared and greeting students at the door instead of scrambling to prepare materials. He preferred to know what the class agenda and expectations were ahead of time, whether that meant the teacher had already established a daily class routine or the schedule was posted or announced at the beginning of class. Teachers who were unable to communicate the schedule or didn't prioritize sticking to a schedule made him feel uncomfortable.

Ben also found that a well-managed classroom deters bullying. Teasing and bullying distract students from learning and functioning well in an academic environment of increasing responsibilities. Ben's favorite teacher was his seventh-grade English teacher, who was caring, didn't "play favorites," and made her classroom a "strict learning atmosphere where things never got out of control, and there was no bullying." Teachers with well-managed classrooms offer their autistic students a comfortable place to interact with others and to learn. Ben describes this feeling of safety as having someone on his side. This teacher cared about his specific learning needs and knew he was teased a lot outside of her class. She made sure her classroom was a safe learning environment for Ben because she knew he needed it to be.

How will you know whether or not your child is placed in a well-managed classroom, and what can you do to intervene if not? Ben believes this will reveal itself once you begin looking further into any issues your child encounters in school. He struggled academically in classes that lacked daily structure, routine, or predictable assessment schedules. His constant complaints of teasing and his poor grades both indicated problems with his learning environment and his inability to adapt. His advice to parents is to sit down and talk to the student's teacher. Parents can ask what a typical day in the class looks like and where the teacher sees their child struggling. The answers to these questions could offer a valuable perspective about the type of academic environment your child needs to be successful. If these investigations signal a classroom management concern, parents should address this with their child's school.

COMMUNICATING WITH THE SCHOOL

Ben also suggests that parents request to have their child removed from a particular class if there is a better available option. If the school rejects the transfer, parents can ask for a plan to help their child succeed. For example, if the problem is related to bullying, the principal or guidance counselor might talk to the classroom teacher, the bullies, and their parents.

"Autism has made me who I am today. Diagnosis is a key to help kids and parents. I find it [the emphasis on a cure] a little offensive because I don't think it is anything that can be cured. But if you were severely affected by it, then I would recommend parents seek out help."

RAPPORT

Another crucial component of Ben's academic success was developing rapport with his teachers. At the private school he attended, he trusted his teachers and resource professionals to offer supports that were in his best interests. He felt like he could go to them with any concerns he had and his problems would be addressed. During the time he attended his local public school, he didn't feel this same level of trust. "There were a lot of other kids with IEPs, and it was as if the special education teachers thought, Ben is fine, he can handle himself, when I was actually really struggling." It helped him to have a teacher who would check in with him periodically to make sure he was grasping material and keeping up with the workload.

Brian King (see Chapter Nine) agrees that a teacher's relationship with an autistic student is vital to that child's success. Teachers need to find out what the child's experience has been in school. He says, "You may be working with a child who has trust issues because of his or her predecessors. You have to let that child know it is going to be different with you. That you are a new character in their story."

NO PLACE LIKE HOME

Even when classrooms are set up to welcome and accommodate autistic students, Ben cautions that the school routine often remains exhausting, partly because of the unpredictability of certain parts of the day (e.g., the lunchroom, the restroom, transitions between classes). The home environment can be more controlled and more comfortable, however. "Home was the one place that I knew no one would make fun of me or pick on me or bully me. It was the safe place where I could do what I wanted and be myself."

Individuals on the spectrum often find socialization in settings outside of the home more tiring than other children do, which is why they need to have a reliable safe zone. If children come home to an environment where they are constantly yelled at or corrected, this can contribute to exhaustion and potential depression.

Ben's advice to parents is that while they must correct, encourage, or otherwise parent their children, they should also try to recognize that their children generally experience more stress during the school day than most NT children. "So try to back off a bit," Ben recommends, "Delay any orders or critiques until your child has settled in. After school (or any outing), autistic children may need time and space to relax before receiving more direction on what they should or shouldn't be doing."

Scheduled relaxation. Ben believes his parents did a good job of balancing the need to work around the house while still allowing him the opportunity to relax in activities of his choosing. Most parents do this to some degree with their children – delaying leisure activities until a chore is completed, for example. Ben recalls that in elementary school, he was fascinated with a television show called Rescue 911. The show featured reenactments of actual 911 calls. He loved emergency vehicles and rescue workers and spent his free time learning as much as possible about this line of work. He knew exactly what time the show came on television in the evening, and his parents used this viewing time as an incentive for completing his homework and doing household chores.

Ben also enjoyed playing board games as another way to relax. This was a great opportunity to practice the social skills of taking turns, negotiating, managing the emotions of winning and losing, and playing by the rules. Family game nights were scheduled events Ben eagerly participated in. He was internally motivated to join his siblings and play the game, and his parents could gently coach him to successfully strategize, work cooperatively, and be a good sport.

The comfort of a routine someone enjoys creates a foundation for developmental success. Ben believes the social confidence he has today is a result of always having a safe and comfortable home base. "I'm not afraid of my social skills being an issue. I enjoy socializing more than I fear any awkward interactions. I don't feel the need to exclude myself anymore."

Creating a safe and comfortable home for your autistic child. There are plenty of organizational and design choices that can make your home more comfortable for your autistic child. Below are a few tips to help your child stay organized and confident within your home:

▸▸ Allow your child to choose the paint color in his bedroom.

▶▶ Give your child regular responsibilities.

▶▶ Use soft or adjustable lighting.

▶▶ Avoid using strong fragrances.

▶▶ Allow a space for exercise (e.g., trampoline, punching bag, open space in a basement with gymnastics mats).

▶▶ Allow your child to customize his bedroom space to suit any particular relaxation needs without sharing with a sibling, if possible.

▶▶ Try to follow a regular meal routine.

▶▶ Create consistency wherever possible with well-organized rooms and visual schedules. (Wang, 2010)

REFLECTION QUESTIONS

▶▶ Which classes does your child succeed in and in which does he struggle? Does the answer to these questions change or remain the same from year to year? What are some possible causes for this? Are they related to classroom management or a particular content area?

▶▶ How might your child benefit from preferential classroom seating to either maintain engagement level or prevent teasing?

▶▶ How can you establish a productive and comfortable after-school schedule for your child? How can you help your child prepare for changes in this schedule?

Chapter Four

Social Manuals, Executive Functioning, and Meditation

AN INTERVIEW WITH TIM PAGE

I don't like apologizing for who I am.

TIM PAGE

SURVIVING KICKBALL WITH OPERA

"I feel like a permanent outsider," Tim Page admits. In his article in The New Yorker entitled "Parallel Play," Tim explains, "[My life] has been spent in a perpetual state of parallel play, alongside, but distinctly apart from, the rest of humanity" (2007, para. 5). Although he can now healthily manage this feeling of separation from society, social ostracization and isolation confused and overwhelmed him when he was growing up, and to help cope, he learned to self-medicate at an early age. For example, at age 2, Tim discovered that opera music helped him escape the confusion and hurt of the world. But the notes weren't just an escape – they captivated him. When the world became too much for little Tim to handle, he ran to his mother's selection of records and found something to calm him down or give him a sense of well-being. And he continued to engage with music as he grew older, even though other kids his age did not seem to share his passion.

> *"You're hurt a lot when you're an autistic kid because you really don't understand, and I wanted company desperately, and it was just very tough for me to learn how to get that company and get on with people."*

While his peers enjoyed playing sports, Tim preferred studying, making his own films, and composing music. In elementary school, he hated gym class. He was awkward and clumsy, unable to coordinate movements that would make him successful in the physical activities his peers enjoyed. Tim dreaded these mandatory activities.

One day he was required to participate in a game of kickball. Waiting in line for his turn to kick, his palms sweat and his heart raced. He watched as one-by-one the kids in front of him made swift contact with the ball and sped to first base. They would turn to home plate and clap encouragement for the next kid in line.

Tim felt the athletic pressure to perform and keep the game going. He also felt the social pressure to act "normal" and enjoy the game as much as his peers did. His throbbing head and tight muscles fought against his chance at the perfect kick to move the base runners, or any play to secure him on first base. When he approached home plate for his turn to kick, the kids in the field relaxed their stances and began taunting him. With each missed kicking attempt, they laughed and called him names. His teammates – stranded on base – rolled their eyes and eventually snickered their lack of faith. After strike three, even his gym teacher piped in, saying, "It's okay Tim, just go home and listen to your opera records." The whole field laughed, bonding over their shared amusement at his expense. Tim left the plate. Then he went home to listen to his opera records.

"[Some teachers] were real out and out bullies."

But the torment wasn't limited to the kickball field. Tim also struggled in the classroom, failing in the classes of teachers who favored him as well as those who encouraged his public humiliation. He began self-educating by the age of 10 at the local library. He couldn't find a comfortable place in a formal educational setting, and his miserable scores kept him at the bottom of his class until 10th grade when he dropped out of school.

Diagnosis: "Back then no one would have said someone as verbal as I was could possibly be autistic. They basically wrote me off as a 'bad kid'"- because how come my IQ was so high? How come I could learn certain things and couldn't do all this other stuff?"

After taking the high school equivalency exam at 19, Tim finally began a positive academic track. He was able to spend two years at a music school studying his interests and was even accepted into a writing class at Columbia University in New York City. Then came an academic break. Columbia accepted him as a full-time student based on his success in his writing class.

During his time at Columbia, Tim was careful to select classes taught by teachers known for having liberal grading procedures or subjects he was already knowledgeable about and skilled in, like music, writing, and film. He had come to a point in his life where people finally started appreciating his unique skill sets rather than ostracizing him for them. Tim had gone from being a high school dropout to an Ivy Leaguer. He graduated with promising opportunities for careers that matched his interests and talents.

But as Tim entered adulthood, something still wasn't quite right. "I had been very successful at squirrely, solitary jobs like becoming a music critic and a writer, where I didn't really have to deal with people except on my own terms. I did most of my work alone." But he couldn't connect in other professional circles. After starting a family and taking a job as an administrator for the St. Louis Symphony in his mid-forties, all of the horrible social anxiety he experienced as a kid came back. He struggled with communication in this new leadership position, having to guess what people were thinking and forcing uncomfortable eye contact with coworkers. The confusion and stress drove him away from this position and to a writing job at The Washington Post.

Similar issues seemed to plague his middle son, and Tim eventually sought the help of a therapist. Tim's son spent years visiting a therapist who labeled him with attention deficit hyperactivity disorder (ADHD) and schizophrenia in an attempt to sort out his complex mood swings, depression, and anxiety. But one day in his office, after several years of faulty guesses and failed treatments, the therapist finally claimed to have the answer. He began describing to Tim's son a neurological condition called Asperger Syndrome (AS), citing symptoms such as (a) social communication challenges, including difficulty with interpreting social cues; and (b) interests in topics with an intensity that often lend themselves to social isolation. The therapist finished his description, then turned to Tim, saying, "And you have it, too."

USING SOCIAL MANUALS TO ADOPT APPROPRIATE SOCIAL BEHAVIOR

Although Tim's social anxiety, confusion, and loneliness impacted both his childhood and adulthood, he still found channels to achieve incredible professional success. Tim used his writing and music talents to become an author and Pulitzer Prize-winning music critic. And while his current professional success is closely tied to being autistic, this neurological condition has also caused him tremendous anxiety and loneliness.

"I'm convinced that my autism has certainly bedeviled me and has been extremely painful an awful lot of the time, but I would agree with the autistic-lib people that there is no way I would have done things like write a book in a summer, or immerse myself in something so completely that I forget about the world, without it."

In talking about his difficulty interpreting social cues, Tim notes that he found it crucial to find a guidebook or some other resource with descriptions of why these otherwise unwritten social rules exist. "It would be easier for me to improvise an epic poem before a sellout crowd at Madison Square Garden than to approach an attractive stranger across the room and strike up a conversation" (Page, 2009, pp. 176-177).

The biggest contributor to his social survival was no other than Emily Post, whose classic book, Etiquette (Post, Post, Post, & Post Senning, 2011), he found on his mother's bookshelf. Fueled by an adolescent craving to gain positive attention from girls, Tim discovered that if the purpose of a rule was explained logically, he could study and internalize it. "I think I've learned a language of emotion, which did not come any more naturally to me than speaking German would for a lot of people."

"Even though it was the most miserable part of my life, what brought me into the real world was puberty because - all of the sudden - I desperately wanted to be around girls and all of the stuff that I was so interested in was not exactly, as they say on the tv show, chick magnet stuff."

Because these social and emotional rules were so foreign to Tim, he needed to develop an approach that was similar to how most people learn academic material. "The fact that my understanding of affection, comradeship, and human empathy has been hard-won rather than being wired in from the start does not make these feelings less genuine" (Page, 2007, para. 43).

"In part everyone is an actor. I've gotten to be extremely good at playing the public. For me it is very helpful to have rules to understand where you fit."

The Benefits of Using a Social Manual

Autistic people usually learn and practice social rules with conscious effort (Prizant & Fields-Meyer, 2015). Etiquette guides and social skills curricula can help present a more comprehensive list of rules as opposed to solely relying on constant behavior corrections, which may be stressful and embarrassing. Both parents and individuals on the spectrum can use social skills curricula to teach and learn social rules and communication. First impressions weigh heavily in so many facets of life. Awkward or negative interactions not only prevent people from making friends, but can also target them for bullying. Unsuccessful first impressions also impact job interviews and dating and limit professional opportunities. Autistic individuals who have difficulty communicating with

NTs may have a frustrating awareness that they cannot control their perceived awkwardness, or they may constantly wonder why they have difficulty making friends or connecting with people. A social guidebook can help prepare them for the situations they want to encounter with more ease and make better impressions with those around them. Written guidebooks are also helpful because they can be a refreshing alternative to the redirection coming from parents or other family members. Well-meaning parents regularly inform their autistic children about society's standards and social rules. While all children grow annoyed with constant parental reprimands, autistic children may become exhausted or overwhelmed when it appears they can't seem to live life "right." Books contain objective, third-party advice that autistic individuals may more readily welcome, especially if they have sought this help on their own. Tim's social success is good news for other individuals on the spectrum. Many autistic people struggle because they are aware of their inability to fit in. Concerned parents or caregivers of autistic children can consider encouraging them to read books on etiquette, like Tim did, if this style matches their preferred learning methods.

EXECUTIVE FUNCTIONING

Tim learned in his professional life that his difficulty with socialization was exacerbated by issues with executive functioning – the mental ability to connect past experiences with present situations, including planning, organizing, predicting, focusing, remembering, managing time, and controlling emotions and impulses (Morin, 2014). One of Tim's jobs later in life was a senior administrator at the St. Louis Symphony Orchestra where he worked with 100 musicians and a staff of 25. "I was a disaster," he says. He couldn't handle the "numerous extra-musical facets of the job." They didn't interest him, and he couldn't pay attention to them. "Not wouldn't," he emphasizes, "couldn't" (Page, 2009, p. 177). Not surprisingly, he was much more comfortable writing for The Washington Post and in the "solitary, squirrely job of a music critic."

Brian King (see Chapter Nine), similar to many autistic people, also has difficulty with executive functioning; in particular, organization and prioritization. For example, he has a hard time figuring out the first and second steps to a project and often enlists the help of his wife or a colleague, or searches Google for templates or systems he can adopt. This strategy makes his life more comfortable because his brain isn't constantly worrying about creating new ideas and systems every time he needs to complete a task.

Jodie Van de Wetering (see Chapter Five) explains that the ways she copes with executive functioning issues go above and beyond what a neurotypical person would need. "It is disheartening sometimes that I need three timers, a whiteboard, and endless reminders and checklists to achieve what other people seem to be able to do with nothing more than a slim diary." But she refuses to compare herself with other people or prioritize looking "sleek and elegant," and instead, reminds herself to focus on getting the job done and what she needs to do so.

The National Center for Learning Disabilities notes that children who have problems with executive functioning may experience the following difficulties:

▸▸ Planning complex projects;

▸▸ Comprehending how much time a project will take to complete;

▸▸ Struggling to communicate details in an organized, sequential manner in both verbal and written stories;

▸▸ Memorizing and retrieving information from memory;

▸▸ Initiating activities or tasks, or generating ideas independently; and

▸▸ Working memory. (Morin, 2014)

Parents can seek out supports that address underlying executive functioning issues rather than only focusing on their symptoms. There are many books, such as FLIPP the Switch: Strengthen Executive Function Skills (Wilkins & Burmeister, 2015), available to help students and their parents target and address specific types of executive functioning issues.

MEDITATION

One strategy Tim learned to help cope with the demands of executive functioning he discovered after a break-up with his girlfriend at age 20. Tim felt an intense loss after the break-up, but he refused to let it destroy him. At the recommendation of a friend, he attended a seminar on meditation to reduce the social and emotional stress he was experiencing. Meditative activity allowed him to relax and significantly diminished his anxiety. "The biggest therapeutic help for me was learning to meditate," says Tim. He believes it gave him the strength to act more independently and take risks, like applying to music school, taking a writing course at Columbia, earning a college degree, and moving to New York to work for The New York Times.

Meditation and Autism

Most of the evidence of the health benefits of meditation is anecdotal; however, proponents claim meditation activates the prefrontal cortex of the brain, which is the area that increases flexibility, the desire to socialize, and the ability to adjust to change (Fierberg, 2016). Meditation can also help reduce the anxiety associated with social communication and behaviors that many individuals with ASD experience. In an article published in Everyday Health, Orenstein (2014) describes meditation as a "no-cost, drug-free therapy" that can help autistic children.

Several organizations, including the National Institutes of Health, American Medical Association, American Psychological Association, and Harvard Medical School, are currently studying the possible benefits of meditation. A review article on meditation as a potential therapy for autism published in the Autism Research and Treatment Journal concluded that meditation, as well as yoga, is a useful health intervention for children ages 3-14 (Sequeira & Ahmed, 2012).

REFLECTION QUESTIONS

▶▶ How can I offer social skills advice or support in a way that matches my child's learning style and isn't mere lecturing?

▶▶ What specific executive functioning tasks does my child find especially difficult?

▶▶ In what ways can I support my child to learn how to self-manage on a daily basis?

▶▶ Is meditation a feasible intervention for my child? What information or support would I (or my child) need to give meditation a try?

Chapter Five

Motor Planning, Sensory Processing, and Cognitive Behavioral Therapy

AN INTERVIEW WITH JODIE VAN DE WETERING

> *I'm not a very trusting person and am also very reluctant to look for or ask for help when I need it. I don't know how much of this is just human nature and how much is because during incidents when I did need help, there was none forthcoming.*
>
> JODIE VAN DE WETERING

THE TRAMPOLINE

Trampolines have a tendency to either accentuate one's athletic abilities or highlight a lack of coordination. Unfortunately for Jodie Van de Wetering, an Australian on the spectrum, trampolines placed her in the latter category. When Jodie's middle-school gym class practiced trampolining one semester, she couldn't hide her motor deficits. She couldn't even hoist herself up onto the trampoline to attempt a jump. There was no step stool available, and no one offered her a hand.

"I was angry because I was obviously having difficulty, but no one around me helped. The other kids laughed, and the teacher kept repeating the same instructions over again." Her peers launched themselves onto the trampoline with ease, but Jodie had to haul herself up like "a graceless sack of spuds." Her efforts entertained her peers, further humiliating her with the reminder that she was different from them. She was already teased for her awkward gait and exploited for her sensitive startle reflex. The trampoline exercise provided a more formal platform for this ridicule. Further fueling her embarrassment, Jodie faced an even more daunting task once she finally reached the top of the trampoline: She had to land on her stomach and jump back to her feet. "This move completely defeated me," Jodie explains. Her body would not let her land on her face. When it became clear that Jodie was unable to complete the move, her teacher told her to try a modified move, falling instead onto her hands and knees before landing on her stomach and then popping back to her feet again. Although the teacher's modification was meant to be helpful, it was not offered in a way Jodie felt comfortable with, amid her snickering peers. Jodie's teacher lacked the foresight to predict Jodie's difficulty and failed to support her appropriately by ignoring the taunting of her peers.

> *Bullying: "I did feel utterly humiliated during the trampoline incident - I was very aware of how different I was from the other kids, and of their reactions."*

Motor Challenges and Autism

Like Jodie, many autistic people have difficulty planning and coordinating physical movements, a condition also known as dyspraxia. This may result in an awkward gait, difficulty playing sports, or general clumsiness (Patino, 2014). They may have trouble perceiving where their body is in space or where on their bodies they are touched. Additionally, people with a specific type of dyspraxia, verbal dyspraxia, have trouble coordinating muscles for speaking, chewing, and swallowing. If these issues go unaddressed, affected people can become overwhelmed with daily organizational tasks such as preparing for school or work-related activities and efficiently managing their time. Traditionally, sensory and motor issues for people on the spectrum have received less attention than other areas of challenges, but professors from Rutgers University and Indiana University recently used a National Science Foundation grant to study and develop a tool to measure minute body fluctuations that may help with autism diagnostics and therapy (Minute Movements, 2014). The technology tracks changes in movements and compares them to patterns of typically developing children. This tool could potentially diagnose children at earlier ages instead of relying on deficit models, which require a wait and see approach. Earlier diagnosis means an earlier opportunity for interventions and supports.

THE CAUSE OF MOTOR PLANNING ISSUES AND WAYS TO ADDRESS THEM

As a result of these experiences, Jodie avoided any exercises or physical activity, which is unfortunate, as exercises might actually have improved her motor planning abilities. "I know that's not healthy, long-term," she admits, "but when you have a finite amount of energy and mental processing to budget, it's easy to leave your physical health at the bottom of the list."

Jodie recommends that people on the spectrum who experience motor issues seek the advice of professionals, such as occupational therapists, who can address sensory needs within a program for developing these skills. "I recommend starting young rather than waiting till you're nearly 30 like I did, when behavioral patterns are much harder to break."

ADDRESSING SENSORY PROCESSING ISSUES

Jodie believes it is important to address sensory processing issues before addressing any other perceived physical or social deficits. One approach she has found especially helpful was identifying specific weaknesses and sensory sensitivities through surveys and discussion and, subsequently, addressing them with a therapist.

Jodie believes identifying and addressing sensory issues is an essential starting point to any therapeutic approach for autism because sensory sensitivities control a person's perception of and interactions with the world.

> I feel there is perhaps too much emphasis – in terms of both research and therapy – on the social skills aspect of the condition, because that is what other people can see. They can't see the pain caused by our sensory sensitivities, for instance. But from personal experience, the social skills stuff is much easier when the sensory sensitivities are under control, because it's hard to be sociable when you're in pain.

Since sensory needs vary from person to person, Jodie found individualized sensory therapy (often led by an occupational therapist) to be much more effective than group therapy. Additionally, general social skills approaches to therapy are most effective if they are able to uncover the true source of a person's discomfort and provide them with the appropriate supports to manage the anxiety and stress they encounter in these social situations.

Jodie recommends talking to the therapists who may be working with your child and discussing the sensory approaches they will use in their sessions. Parents can set up a loving, supportive, comfortable atmosphere for their children at home, and, during therapy sessions, communicate what has worked in order to address their functional needs and optimize productivity during these times.

COGNITIVE BEHAVIORAL THERAPY

Jodie also participated in cognitive behavioral therapy (CBT) to help her better manage her social life. CBT is a therapeutic approach that assumes behavior is intertwined with how people think and feel, so its aim is to make individuals more aware of how they think and feel, thus enabling them to identify triggers to undesirable behaviors and manage them more effectively (Cognitive Behavioural Therapy, 2015).

CBT involves symptom assessment, patient education, and patient training. It helps patients find appropriate local resources or additional therapies. CBT is used to help those with a variety of conditions, including depression, anxiety, posttraumatic stress disorder (PTSD), and obsessive-compulsive disorder (OCD).

Unfortunately, Jodie didn't think CBT was helpful to her. For example, during her sessions. she was instructed to analyze past situations, which she didn't find relevant. It was too late to change her emotions or reactions, so she could not see the purpose of the exercise. Although she could identify in hindsight the behaviors she wanted to change, she still had difficulty applying this knowledge to future situations. The process she was taught was far too complicated for her to remember and apply in real-time situations.

Jodie asserts that the more input an individual has in choosing any therapy increases its chance for effectiveness. More specifically, the individual's role in defining the problems that are addressed in CBT or any therapy is an important factor in the particular therapy's effectiveness.

Defining her own challenges made an important difference for Jodie, especially once she identified some of her sensory sensitivities. She realized how important it was to address her sensory issues since they were so integrated with how she perceived her world. "Social skills are actually relatively low on the list of things I'd like addressed in order to have a happier and more productive life, but they're the first (and usually only) thing therapists want to talk about."

Diagnosis: "My own first emotion was incredible relief. I'd known there was something 'wrong' with me for a long, long time, and finally having a name for it and an understanding of it that made sense – in a way that anxiety or depression just didn't – was probably just as therapeutic as any actual therapy. Having a name for it also meant I was able to discover the autistic community online, which has been a massive help."

REFLECTION QUESTIONS

▶▶ What activities might your child enjoy that would help develop motor skills while also offering opportunities for socialization?

▶▶ What types of sensory sensitivities does your child have that could potentially be aggravated in a therapy session?

▶▶ Has your child taken a sensory inventory? How do you help your child address sensory issues in new environments?

Chapter Six

"Correcting" Autistic Behavior and the Ethical Challenges of Autism Therapy

AN INTERVIEW WITH KATHY GRAY

> *It's like someone took your identity and smashed it with a sledge hammer and now you have all of these pieces ... but then you realize that it explains a lot and that it is the missing piece of who I am.*

KATHY GRAY ON HER DIAGNOSIS OF PDD-NOS

WHAT I LEARNED FROM DISNEY'S MONORAIL

When Kathy Gray was 8, her mother took her on a dream vacation to the "happiest place on earth:" Disneyland. Upon their arrival, Kathy quickly discovered that her favorite park feature was the purple monorail. She loved that the track hovered above the park and described the various scenes they passed. Over their three-day park adventure, Kathy memorized the entire monorail recording, chiming in with the narrator at each ride, and repeating the script as they visited the rest of the park attractions. She talked about the monorail wherever they went and even made up a song about her new fascination.

Kathy's mother didn't share the same enthusiasm for the monorail. Kathy recalls her asking, "Do you have to talk about the monorail all the time? Do you talk like this to your friends at school?" Kathy felt bad about upsetting her mother and began crying. She was embarrassed and couldn't understand what she had done wrong, but she knew talking about the monorail was now off-limits. She was no longer able to enjoy the vacation as freely as she desired. "I sort of felt stupid that I made Mom upset for going on and on and on about it. That aspect of my vacation was put into a corner of my brain labeled: fixations that must die because talking about them made Mom upset."

It wasn't until much later in life that Kathy was able to reflect analytically on this experience. She now understands why she has a tendency to talk at length about her topics of interest. "I *do* have to talk about my fixation or special interest because my brain is stuck, but this can be channeled and redirected appropriately. Unfortunately, in 1993 when all this was taking place, only Temple Grandin, [world-renowned autistic author and livestock industry consultant] and a handful of autism specialists recognized that." Kathy also realized her true friends accepted her quirks and that, therefore, she didn't feel the need to forcibly monitor her conversations or avoid certain topics for fear of annoying them.

Once when Kathy was working with other autistic people in a group home, one of her clients reminded her of the joy she had experienced on that Disneyland vacation. He showed her a box full of familiar, purple-lined train cars and pieces of elevated tracks. "I was reminded of my fixation, but instead of feeling shame, I felt a connection to my client." She readily agreed to help her client put the monorail track together and shared his enthusiasm in the process.

HOW TO APPROPRIATELY CORRECT AUTISTIC BEHAVIOR

At Disneyland, Kathy was confused by her mother's irritation over her overzealous monorail interest, but felt she had to avoid the subject. As an adult, Kathy is better able to articulate her frustration with incidents like these. For example, she points out that yelling at her when she is excited or fixated on something is not helpful. If someone has a desire to adapt to a particular NT setting and an interest is interfering with success, then that person can learn appropriate ways for channeling this excitement.

Don't make a scene. When Kathy was embarrassed or scared because her mother scolded her in the presence of strangers, she got distracted from whatever her mother was trying to communicate by retreating to safer behaviors of remaining quiet or still. A better approach for parents who feel that a behavior needs to be changed would be to offer suggestions or corrections, but avoid making a public scene.

Use children's special interests. A positive way to capitalize on children's fixations and special interests is to use them to motivate academic and social pursuits. In Uniquely Human, the authors explain the importance of intense interests: "Though they come with challenges, enthusiasms often represent the greatest potential for people with autism" (Prizant & Fields-Meyer, 2015, p. 70). Parents and teachers can use a passion to motivate a child to be more socially engaged and develop problem-solving skills (Prizant & Fields-Meyer, 2015). For example, Kathy's teachers could have used her love of the monorail to teach her mathematical story problems. Or maybe a monorail set could have been used to teach her important social skills, such as sharing, taking turns, and initiating and maintaining conversation.

"I want to see them [special interests] as tools, not view them as reasons I was punished. I don't want them to be a source of shame."

Kathy's teachers never engaged her this way, but luckily she had relatives who would talk with her at length about her special interests without making her feel bad for having them. Her uncle, for example, used the metaphor of a webpage to encourage her to branch out and build off her special interest to learn new things. Kathy's special interest at the time was John F. Kennedy. Her uncle pointed out that she could learn about other things related to President Kennedy, such as the government or life in the 1960s and consider these subtopics as links on the larger President Kennedy webpage she was so interested in.

If autistic children have interests that interfere with daily functioning, their parents can seek help coaching them to learn new skills while still acknowledging whatever excites them. Intense passion, focus, and hard work can be commendable traits when channeled to achieve many successes in life.

Acknowledge children's behaviors and feelings. As part of correcting a child's behavior, Kathy stresses the importance of acknowledging how the child is feeling. Working with adult males on the spectrum living in a group home, Kathy addressed aggressive behaviors by communicating her understanding of their frustration before explaining why a given behavior was not permitted, saying things like, "I understand you are frustrated right now, but you can't throw or kick things because it isn't safe." She also encourages her clients to use sign language as a replacement behavior for aggression to communicate their desires. Acknowledging good behaviors helps people on the spectrum understand that not everything they do has to be corrected or changed. It's important for them to know that people see the good things they do and all of the efforts they make on a daily basis.

THE ETHICAL CHALLENGES
OF AUTISM THERAPY

A variety of therapy interventions are widely used with individuals with autism, including occupational therapy (OT), speech-language therapy (ST), physical therapy (PT), cognitive behavior therapy (CBT), social skills training, and applied behavior analysis (ABA). Kathy warns that some of these interventions are not always respectful or productive. In general, however, Kathy believes therapy is an important intervention for many individuals on the spectrum, but it is her observation that ethical challenges exist in the implementation of autism therapy that should be acknowledged.

Lydia Wayman (see Chapter Seven) agrees. Lydia says her experience with behavior therapy was "a nightmare" – "The success or failure of this type of therapy [ABA] depends entirely on the person writing the goals."

Kathy recommends that therapists be sensitive to how they enforce behaviors that an autistic person may find stressful, such as eye contact. Grandin and Panek (2014) discussed the neurological patterns of autistic brains that may explain why autistic people have difficulty with eye contact:

> A 2011 fMRI [functional MRI] study in the Journal of Autism and Developmental Disorders found that the brains in a sample of high-functioning autistics and typically developing individuals seemed to respond to eye contact in opposite fashions. In the neurotypical brain, the right temporoparietal junction (TPJ) was active to direct gaze, while in the autistic subject, the TPJ was active to averted gaze. Researchers think that the TPJ is associated with social tasks that include judgments of others' mental states. The study found the opposite pattern in the left dorsolateral prefrontal cortex: in neurotypicals, activation to averted gaze; in autistics, activation to direct gaze. So it's not that autistics don't respond to eye contact, it's that their response is the opposite of neurotypicals.' (p. 35)

Again, citing from the study, Grandin and Panek (2014) concluded:

> What a neurotypical person feels when someone won't make eye contact might be what a person with autism feels when someone does make eye contact. And vice versa: What a neurotypical feels when someone does make eye contact might be

what an autistic feels when someone doesn't make eye contact. (pp. 35-36)

Eye contact can be uncomfortable and confusing for people on the spectrum. Angela Andrews (see Chapter Twelve) also articulates this discomfort, "Looking in [other people's eyes] makes my stomach turn." Rozella Stewart summarized the eye contact and autism controversy in her article, "Should We Insist on Eye Contact With People Who Have Autism Spectrum Disorders?" saying, "Sometimes getting an individual to 'make eye contact' becomes a high priority that falls under the rubric of 'compliance and direction following' training" (n.d., para. 6). Yet, autistic adults and their families rarely report that eye contact is a useful means of communicating. Stewart cited several anecdotes, one from a man diagnosed with autism who said, "If you insist that I make eye contact with you, when I'm finished I'll be able to tell you how many millimeters your pupils changed while I looked into your eyes" (n.d., para. 7).

> *Despite the widespread enthusiasm for ABA as an effective autism support, there exists an undercurrent of resistance to this approach, largely from autistic self-advocates. For some, the problem doesn't lie in the philosophy behind behaviorism or ABA itself, but in how it is often executed. Underscoring this distinction, Amy Gravino (see Chapter Eight) explains, "ABA is like ice cream. There are lots of flavors – different ways to teach it." This is true for ABA as well as all other autism therapy interventions.*

A significant ethical challenge with regard to therapy is the power differential surrounding the planning and execution of therapy sessions. If autistic individuals have not voluntarily signed up for a particular therapy, then someone else is determining what their needs are. Like many others, Kathy was fortunate as she sought out the help of a psychologist who was able to offer her answers to questions she had about social behavior. She visited the psychologist on a weekly basis after her diagnosis, and then transitioned to seeing her once monthly. The therapist helped her process social life during her transition into adulthood, understanding why people acted the way they did. She found this type of therapy effective because she had control over what was discussed. She appreciated being listened to and supported by her therapist rather than being reprimanded, dismissed, or ignored as had been the case with peers and adults in her life.

A Note on ABA Therapy

Kathy never received ABA, but this is a common therapy for children on the spectrum that many autistic adults condemn. ABA entered the public awareness in 1987 when Dr. O. Ivar Lovaas published a landmark study regarding the gains 19 preschool children had made after intense behavioral intervention. By age 7, the group receiving the therapy had less restrictive school placements and higher IQs than the control group. After a follow-up study in 1993, evidence suggested that behavior therapy may produce lasting gains for children on the autism spectrum (McEachin, Smith, & Lovaas, 1993). A more recent study conducted in Europe followed 15 families who implemented a home-based ABA program and reported positive gains in social skills, problem behaviors, communication, motor skill development, and quality of life, among other areas (McPhilemy & Dillenburger, 2013). The cost of most behavior programs is significant, since an intensive program can include 20-40 hours of therapy a week (Kalmeyer, 2010). Because of the scientific evidence documented on ABA outcomes and other behavioral therapy models, 39 states have adopted autism insurance reform laws requiring insurance companies to share in the cost of therapy (Autism Speaks, n.d.). Despite what some interpret as positive publicized results from ABA-related studies, there is much ethical debate in the way the therapy is executed, especially among the autistic community.

NATURAL ENVIRONMENT TEACHING (NET)

One disadvantage of clinic-based therapy is that the skill is not practiced in the environment where the behavior naturally occurs. While some people may need formal therapy, Kathy says there are plenty of benefits to be gained from informal experiences, such as exposure to peer groups in regular play dates or even in the day-to-day interactions with a sibling. Setting up these more natural situations offers valuable life experiences in a more comfortable environment.

Shawna Hinkle (see Chapter Ten) dislikes clinic-based ABA, preferring ABA to be implemented in a setting "where it's more normalized and not robotic." Natural environment teaching (NET) is one example of such an approach. NET therapy can be held in the child's home or in a public space such as a library, church, park, or grocery store (Potterfield, 2013). The goal is to help individuals learn skills in the settings where they will be used to ensure the skills are mastered for practical applications. As such, the NET therapist uses the child's interests as a guide for instruction and incorporates lessons into the child's regular activities.

LISTENING TO OUR CHILDREN

Parents of nonverbal children often speak of the surprising things they learn about their children when they teach them to use communication boards or voice augmentation and speech-generating devices (SGDs). If parents can misinterpret something as basic as a favorite color (as Winslet and Ericsdottir describes in The Golden Hat: Talking Back to Autism [2012]), they are likely to misunderstand an opinion regarding the intricacies of a particular therapy regimen.

Parents of verbal autistics may have an easier time understanding their children's passions and frustrations, but they still must practice empathy and try not to lose sight of the fact that their children may have different needs and priorities than they do.

REFLECTION QUESTIONS

▶▶ How can your child's special interest be transformed or channeled into something productive (if it isn't already)? What steps do you need to take?

▶▶ In what ways can you advocate for your child in public where other adults may be judging you or your child's behavior?

▶▶ What behaviors would you like your child to change? Why?

▶▶ How does your child feel when attempting to maintain eye contact?

Forging Relationships
AN INTERVIEW WITH LYDIA WAYMAN

I want people to know that a bubbly, intelligent, pretty girl can be different, even 'diagnosably' so, and that there is nothing wrong with my neurology.

LYDIA WAYMAN

IT'S NOT WHAT YOU DID. IT'S YOU!

After Lydia Wayman's autism diagnosis at age 21, a lifetime of confusing and difficult situations came together. One of these situations was the sudden ending of a valued long-term friendship. Through her childhood, Lydia succeeded academically, and she was content with one close friend and occasional playtime with other kids who also didn't quite fit in, but when cliques started to form in the eighth grade, she began to struggle. Understanding social patterns in relationships confused her, and it became harder to make and keep friends.

> Diagnosis: "I can't help but think that, had we had a name for all of my rigidity, my anxiety, my unusual social tones, that things might have been different. I don't blame autism for what happened, but I do blame the lack of awareness of what autism really looks like, especially in women, for the difficulties I had before my diagnosis."

Lydia spent most of her childhood playtime with one friend; let's call her "Stephanie." Lydia had known Stephanie since kindergarten; they usually saw each other six days a week, and shared many interests. When they entered high school, they both decided they wanted to be doctors. After their sophomore year, they had the opportunity to attend a national leadership forum for students who were interested in pursuing careers in the medical field. At the conference, Stephanie met a boy whom she became excited about and wanted to spend a lot of time with. This upset and confused Lydia. She thought, Boys? We don't get involved with those ... What is she doing? This was the first sign things were beginning to change between them.

A few months later, another incident happened that further separated the pair. Lydia was a member of the color guard at school, and while enjoying it, she often felt overwhelmed by the large group and the complex social structure. One day, Lydia was unfairly singled out by the captain in front of the whole group and told that she couldn't march at homecoming. Lydia has Type 1 diabetes, which means that she sometimes has to take snack breaks. The captain said Lydia would ruin their routine if she were to stop and get out a hard candy to suck on while twirling. Stephanie defended her, but finally said to Lydia, "They've been acting like this since we started two years ago – it's not like they're going to change now. Are you sure you shouldn't quit? It's not fair to you."

Eventually Lydia did quit the color guard, but Stephanie began distancing herself shortly after the incident. When she visited her friend's house, Lydia found herself spending more time with Stephanie's younger sister while Stephanie wandered off to do something else.

Later that school year, their friendship ended with Stephanie explaining, "I'm done. I will always care for you and love you, but our friendship is over, and I want no more contact with you." Lydia notes, "It wasn't what I did, it was who I am that was the problem."

For months afterwards, Lydia respected this request although she was completely confused by it. Stephanie maintained her spot in their social circle while Lydia was pushed to the outskirts, forced to travel the social arena alone. Nearly a year later, Lydia tried to reach out and resume their friendship. According to Lydia, this was the worst conversation of her life. Stephanie yelled at her, blamed her for ruining her life, and concluded by pronouncing that she didn't care if Lydia died and that ditching her was the best thing she had ever done.

Not surprisingly, this was devastating to Lydia and made her doubt whether she would ever be able to love or trust anyone again. Indeed, the incident has permanently affected her and prevented future relationships. If she senses something even slightly uncomfortable in a friendship, Lydia begins to withdraw so as to leave before she gets left.

> *"That fallout hit me so hard, cut me so deep, that it may take me the rest of my life to build myself back up. I truly don't know why my friend ditched me, even now."*

On a superficial level, Lydia knew friendships were based on trust, but until that point she hadn't thought about what a friendship looked like in reality. For all those years Lydia had implicitly trusted her friend without thinking about it. After they parted ways, Lydia realized there was so much about social life she didn't understand, and, consequently, she lost confidence in herself as a valuable friend. She didn't trust anyone who wanted to be around her. Lydia figured out that when a relationship has no trust, there is "intense anxiety about the ever-present threat of its failure." She opted for the safety and sadness of solitude instead of the stress involved in a relationship.

> My relationships were completely healthy before my heart got broken. Unusual – yes. Autism-y? You bet. But entirely healthy. That fallout hit me so hard, cut me so deep, that it may take me the rest of my life to build myself back up. I can't help but think that, had we had a name for all of my rigidity, my anxiety, my unusual social tones, that things might have been different. I don't blame autism for what happened, but I do blame the lack of awareness of what autism really looks like, especially in women, for the difficulties I had before my diagnosis.

FORGING RELATIONSHIPS

Finding a neurotypical friend. Lydia says NT friends can help autistic people navigate complex social expectations. In everyday settings and real time, they can explain a pun, warn about upcoming sensory overload, or bridge the gap to meeting new people. They can also give a nudge when a topic has gone on long enough or explain why a word choice may have been heard much differently than it was meant. "I continue to remind myself not to blame the autism, but rather to take responsibility for my actions and reactions and learn to grow through them."

Similarly, it is important to place autistic children in general education settings as much as possible in order to surround them with NT peers. But mere placement among NT peers cannot guarantee academic success. An ideal inclusion setting still acknowledges and supports the unique needs of the autistic student, which may be vastly different than their NT peers. Grandin and Panek remind us that "putting kids who are on the spectrum in the same classroom as their non-autistic peers and treating them the same way is a mistake" (Grandin & Panek, 2014, pp. 182-183). The authors go on to state that this only leads to further marginalization because whoever is different will stand alone. But, whenever possible, an inclusion classroom (with individualized supports) can encourage regular positive peer socialization and friendships while also promoting autism acceptance among NTs (Grandin & Panek, 2014).

Keeping an open mind about types of friendship. While finding an NT friendship can be beneficial, Lydia recommends that parents be open to supporting a variety of relationships for their children. She often hears from parents and teachers that an autistic child only wants to spend time with lower-functioning children while the parents would prefer the child to spend time interacting with NT or nondisabled peers. For Lydia, some of her closest friends are nondisabled, but people have told her these relationships are not genuine, thus placing parameters on her friendships:

> A couple of my closest friends are these kids – we share interests, jokes, and trust. It's really that uncomplicated. I think the world of this kid who's been told it's not really a friendship because I'm an adult and she's a child, and I can't possibly care about her. And the boy she sits with at lunch can't be her friend because she opens his milk. And the boys she plays with after school are, well, they're all boys.

Lydia sees inclusion as "fantastic" if it means that everyone has an equal chance to be part of a community and worthy of friendship. A relationship may look atypical, but it isn't necessarily unhealthy. In a US News and World Report article, "How to Be a Friend to Someone With Autism," Lydia Brown explains that autistic people, like their NT counterparts, desire a variety of friendships. "Like all people, we value others who want to be our friends for the sake of who we are. We seek friendships based on mutual interest and respect, shared values and negotiated boundaries" (Haupt, 2014). Similarly, Lydia asks parents not to place unnecessary limits on their children's friendships and be open to healthy socialization opportunities and relationships from a variety of sources.

Just as NTs who befriend autistics help the people on the spectrum gain confidence and maintain a healthy emotional state, NT parents can also benefit from establishing friendships with autistic adults. In fact, it is a useful first step to take upon discovering your child's diagnosis (Neurodivergent K, 2016). Having an autistic friend can help parents gain unique advice that will benefit their children. Such a relationship also authenticates NT parents' acceptance of autism in the world and models this belief. The autistic child will know his parents value the human dignity of autistic people because he will see his parents in action, connecting as equals, as human adults.

> *Diagnosis: "My mom was very hesitant and questioned the validity of the diagnosis. She spent months just researching before she realized how pervasive autism really was in my life. My dad chose, and continues to choose, to ignore it."*

But Lydia Brown warns that autistic people don't exist as props or perpetual resources for other people. "We have our own lives and goals. It's rather objectifying and dehumanizing to think about autistic adults as existing only for the benefit of non-autistic parents, but not being able to exist in our own right." However, an organic friendship between an autistic adult and a nonautistic parent can help a parent gain confidence in knowing the child can "turn out okay" as an adult, and this situation might provide the child with someone to relate to and look up to.

Amy Gravino (see Chapter Eight) adds that getting to know someone on the spectrum can help NT parents dispel some preconceived ideas about autism and their own child's future. "If you get to know someone who has already walked that path and who understands on a very personal level what your child is going through, that can help you to better help your child as a parent, and develop a greater sense of compassion and understanding as a human being."

IT GETS BETTER

"It gets better," Lydia says. "The pain from youthful torment may subside as you learn to cope in healthy ways after growing older and surrounding yourself with more mature adults." But the transition isn't always an easy or quick one.

"Time is your ticket to self-awareness, confidence, and understanding more about who you are and where you fit into this world." In her case, Lydia struggled through high school knowing that crowds bothered her, noise overwhelmed her, and conversations confused her, but she didn't know diagnostic terms like 'sensory issues' or 'visual processing.' For Lydia, learning about her autism diagnosis helped her to begin making sense of her life.

With time, Lydia has become able to connect with others on the spectrum who accept her needs, specifically her preference for communicating through writing and typing. She once viewed this preference as a personal failure. However, once she connected with others on the spectrum, she learned that typing to communicate was okay. This changed her life, allowing her to find friends and connect in ways she never could before. She even completed her MA in English and Creative Nonfiction online, an education model she says was built for her.

Lydia admits that reminding yourself "it gets better" is not an instant solution to a rough patch; however, time eventually grants opportunities for growth, especially for young adults. "Your environment changes, you have new opportunities to learn and make sense of your life, you can spot the patterns of problems throughout your life and seek solutions. And the biggest impact comes from the thing you control the most – your attitude."

After acclimating to a given environment, individuals on the spectrum can gain the comfort and confidence to make friends and pursue personal interests. Lydia felt most welcome in her church and in the company of women who were 10- to 20-years older than her because they tended to accept people as they are. Today Lydia has a variety of friends both on and off the spectrum, living near and far from her home. Acceptance is key to maintaining friendships. "I belong to a local independent autism center, and I can come in and be asked five times in five minutes about my cat – I love my cat, and my friends ask instead of wishing I would be quiet about it."

While it may be difficult for some autistics to embrace the idea that socialization eventually does get easier, supportive adult role models (or mature peers) can befriend them, love them, and be open to learning from them along the way. Or, as "E" (a Loud Hands contributor) asserts, "No, it doesn't get better. You get stronger. You will always have to be stronger. You will always have to try harder" (cited in Bascom, 2012, p. 129).

REFLECTION QUESTIONS

▶▶ How can you teach or encourage your child to pursue friendships?

▶▶ How can you encourage your child to engage with other autistic communities or particular groups of interest?

▶▶ In what ways are you a good acceptance model for your child?

▶▶ What opportunities do you have to socialize with the autistic community?

Friendship and Sexuality Throughout Adolescence

AN INTERVIEW WITH AMY GRAVINO

Autism is inextricably intertwined with my identity. It's not who I am, but it's a part of who I am. And if I was to get rid of that, I would be getting rid of a huge part of myself. I wouldn't be me without it. And I wouldn't have done all of these things without it. I don't even know what my life would be.

AMY GRAVINO

"IF I DID THIS ONE THING ..."

"I used to feel like a lot of people just didn't care ... that everybody in my world didn't care what was happening to me."

At the end of her senior year, Amy Gravino's high school Latin teacher hosted a pool party for all of her students. Amy was excited to wear the new bikini she had purchased for the occasion. Most girls chose to wear bikinis to stand out, but Amy wanted to wear one to fit in. She was never considered very popular and had difficulty finding friends.

On the day of the party, Amy donned her bikini and eagerly left her home. When she got there, the pool was surrounded by students talking, swimming, playing games, and laughing, so Amy immediately attempted to casually socialize with her classmates. She had a crush on one of the boys and hoped her new bikini would make her worthy of his attention. She smiled and laughed at the appropriate times, even though she didn't quite understand her classmate's humor. Amy thought that as long as she laughed with them, they couldn't laugh at her. But as usual, she was ignored. She felt invisible. Standing outside of the group, which never even glanced in her direction, she had the sudden awareness, "It doesn't matter that I'm wearing this. I still don't belong." It was a harsh realization for someone who had tried her whole life to fit in.

> *"I remember up until then my line of thinking was: What's wrong with all these people- my class, in terms of my peers at school - what's wrong with them, why can't they see things how I do? When puberty started to hit about eleven [or] twelve, it became: What's wrong with me, why can't I see things the way they do?"*

Through middle and high school, Amy had told herself, "If I wear this one kind of make-up, I will fit in ... Maybe if I would wear this particular outfit, I will fit in. I always felt like there was one thing standing between me and finding all these friends, and I kept trying to find it, to circumvent it, and it just never, ever worked."

> *"I would watch my peers, I would imitate exactly what they did, I would do it I thought letter perfect, but because I was the one doing it, I was wrong. No matter how well I thought I did it."*

Although she was teased, this negative attention didn't bother her nearly as much as being ignored. "It was those moments of being in the hall and seeing everyone interact around me, knowing that I couldn't be a part of it, that killed me."

> *"Being ignored- that was almost worse than being picked on. Because when you're being picked on, they are acknowledging you exist, you're there. But when you're being ignored, it's like you're not even there. I mean, I had a classmate tell me to my face that if I disappeared, if I killed myself, nobody would care."*

ACHIEVING A SENSE OF SELF

Amy had to build herself up and figure out who she was after the social confusion she experienced in high school. But she says once you discover who you are, no one can take that away from you. "Walk with your head held high and people will follow." For Amy, this was a gradual process. It took a lot of days of waking up in the morning, looking in the mirror, and choosing to like what she saw. She did not like her body. She would grab a towel immediately after a shower, quickly covering herself so she wouldn't catch a glimpse of her body in the mirror. Eventually, she was able to leave the shower and admire her naked body. This change happened when she made a daily commitment to choose to be strong and to remove herself from the people who made fun of her. "The voice of negativity slowly began to dissipate."

According to Amy, "The key is to develop a strong sense of yourself." Lydia Wayman (see Chapter Seven) agrees. Lydia has friends who want their autism to be cured, and she would never tell them they're wrong for having that desire, but adds, "Personally, I embrace my quirks, and I'm not going to waste my energy on hypotheticals. I would rather spend my time working through my challenges and adapting my surroundings and my attitude in a way that allows me to flourish, rather than on what-ifs."

FINDING SOMEONE WHO UNDERSTANDS

While Amy's socialization problems did not entirely disappear in college, she was able to find friends who understood autism and were willing to accommodate her needs so they could maintain a solid friendship. As a result, Amy continued to gain confidence in her identity as a capable woman on the spectrum.

Due to the high numbers of people diagnosed (1 in 59 according to a 2018 report from the Centers for Disease Control and Prevention), autism is now consistently discussed in the media, and most people have a basic understanding of some of the struggles autistic people face. Surrounding themselves with patient, caring people who are willing to learn, understand, and accommodate helps autistic people thrive in a society that is easier for some NTs to navigate.

In college, Amy found someone in her dorm whose brother had autism and, therefore, understood some of her difficulties. Amy appreciated that she didn't have to explain each of her behaviors to this friend. For example, one evening they visited a restaurant and bar celebrating a beach-themed event. The noise level was too harsh for Amy, so she knelt down in front of a beach display and began playing with the sand, running it through her fingers. Her friend looked down at her and said, "Well, looks like you're a little overwhelmed." Amy was shocked that someone else understood that her behavior stemmed from a sensory overload. Her friend didn't give her a strange look and ask her to stop; she read Amy's cues and could then effectively communicate with her and make her feel more comfortable. She didn't judge or encourage Amy to "tough it out;" she accommodated her.

ESTABLISHING A CONSISTENT, LOVING PRESENCE THROUGHOUT ADOLESCENCE

In school. Amy was supported both at home and in school and believes that the more consistent, positive influences a child experiences in life, the better. Although many of her teachers didn't know how to help her or did not appear to want to, a guidance counselor in elementary school had the patience and concern to be Amy's lifeline. For example, she knew Amy had a fear of thunderstorms, and let her bolt to her office whenever a storm hit during school hours. The counselor also established a routine during Amy's regular visits, such as offering her an English muffin before each of their sessions to make Amy feel more comfortable. These sessions were pivotal during Amy's transition to middle school, offering a stable, caring presence during an otherwise chaotic time in her life.

Based on her personal experience, Amy offers the following advice to teachers, counselors, and paraprofessionals working with autistic students: "To you, this is your job; to us, this is our lives." She wants them to understand that if a student won't behave in the way they expect them to, it isn't personal.

> There were days when it was all I could do to hold myself together, or where I was perseverating on something that happened days prior, and that was causing me to not be able to focus, and so many times, it's things like that that drive student behavior, rather than anything a teacher said or did.

Amy could tell the difference when teachers or counselors engaged with her because it was their job and when they sincerely cared about her. She believes all students are aware of this difference even though they may not be able to express or articulate it. Educational professionals "have the choice to be a positive or negative influence on someone, one that will most certainly stay with them for the rest of their lives."

Maintaining a consistent, supportive parental role is especially important throughout adolescence. The socialization difficulties children experience in elementary school often become more strained in middle and high school when puberty hits. Adolescence is an intimidating time for all parents, and autism can bring additional challenges into the mix. Despite the potentially messy road of adolescence, there is good reason to think that autistics, like most kids, will survive to live a smoother adulthood. Indeed, recent studies show that problem behaviors and daily living skills improve across the spectrum into adulthood (Sarris, 2013). But in the meantime, Amy underscores the importance of parents adopting a solid foundation for their children.

Autism and sexuality. According to Amy, one of the most important sexuality issues people on the spectrum face is that NTs, including parents, therapists, and medical professionals, have false assumptions of autistic sexuality. This includes the idea that autistics aren't having sex, aren't interested in sex, or are hypersexual (sexually promiscuous, deviant, or out-of-control). These assumptions are damaging and often lead to the perception that people on the spectrum are undesirable or easily taken advantage of.

Amy advises parents to support their children during adolescence by empowering them with knowledge and information to make the right decisions for themselves. "Let them know that they can have a choice, that they have worth and value and don't have to automatically go out with the first person who shows interest in them." Don't be afraid to answer their questions. Don't minimize their desires or make them feel ashamed for asking questions. "If you can ease that sense of guilt and self-blame by being someone we can openly talk to and trust, you will have made some part of our lives that much easier and better."

However, Amy cautions not to forget that autistic teenagers are teenagers, "with all of the raging hormones and physical and emotional changes to match. It's entirely too easy to blame everything on autism, when much of what we go through is a truly typical teenage experience." Parents can encourage independence and self-awareness by allowing their children to safely explore relationships with people they are attracted to and by asking their children to examine their own behavior and actions rather than protecting them from all of the negative consequences. "If we are not given the opportunity to develop self-awareness, our sexuality becomes controlled and determined by others instead of ourselves."

Parents or other family members can support autistic teens by "being there for them and listening."

> It's not always what they say that is important, but what they don't say too. This is especially true when puberty and the hormones kick in. Many people shut down. Think about what they didn't tell you during the day. Maybe they only talk about one specific thing that happened, and it is the same each day. Tell them that you are always there if they want to talk. Give them the choice about wanting to talk.

Amy recalls that during her adolescence, she felt like she didn't have control over anything. She felt like everyone had told her what she needed and how she was supposed to think, feel, and act. Autistic teens are no different from their NT counterparts in that they need to be given the freedom to explore their own interests and discover some of their needs for themselves. This gives them ownership of their education, their work, their relationships, and, ultimately, their lives.

Using video modeling and self-modeling for dating. In graduate school, Amy was interested in the sexuality issues of autistic individuals and how she could help people on the spectrum navigate the dating world. As part of her thesis study for her master's degree in applied behavior analysis, Amy researched the effectiveness of video modeling in helping adult males with autism learn how to ask someone out on a date. Amy concluded from her research that video modeling was the best way for her participants to observe their own behaviors and compare them to a "goal" video she had created for the study. "I found it to be very effective as a learning tool, and I think it could be beneficial for individuals both on and off the autism spectrum."

Video modeling consists of an individual demonstrating how to engage in a particular behavior. This evidence-based practice benefits young children, adolescents, and adults with autism and can be used to teach a variety of social, daily living, and employment skills (Wong et al., 2015).

Adolescence Brings New Challenges

Beyond the challenges associated with dating that Amy addressed in her video modeling research, adolescence brings a host of other issues for people on the spectrum. In an article on autistic teenagers published by the Interactive Autism Network, Dr. Michael Rosenthal of the Child Mind Institute discusses the reasons behind some of the challenges adolescent autistics encounter (Sarris, 2013).

Rosenthal's recent research on autistic teens with IQ scores of 70 or higher reveals that they have slower executive functioning maturity, which leads to difficulties organizing time and resources, relating past memories to present experiences, and working effectively in a group. This is particularly troublesome in middle and high school, which present increasing demands on students, both academically and socially. For example, students are expected to switch classes more often, independently keep track of assignments, and navigate unfamiliar social environments or settings less supervised than ever before (e.g., the lunchroom, hallway transitions, recess, and lecture halls).

Because every autistic child is different, each will each have unique adolescent needs and challenges. Some will experience constant frustration with learning new social rules related to personal hygiene or behaviors necessary to gain ground in the dating sphere. Others may face new safety concerns. For example, in a 2013 Huffington Post article, actress Holly Robinson Peete expressed fear that her autistic son who loves the sensory input of a hoodie pulled around his face and his hands tucked into his pockets may attract the suspicion of police. If confronted by a police officer, she worries her son would not be able to communicate quickly enough to diffuse a tense situation. In the article she explains that she introduced her son to local law enforcement, which she hopes will help her son if police ever confront him.

REFLECTION QUESTIONS

▶▶ How can you help your child develop a stronger and more confident identity?

▶▶ What can you do to help your child make or keep friends?

▶▶ What can you do to make your child feel more comfortable coming to you with social concerns and view you as a loving, supportive listener?

▶▶ What new challenges does your adolescent face? How can you support your child in these areas?

Chapter Nine

Redefining Communication
AN INTERVIEW WITH BRIAN KING

I insist on always being a student. I'm always in teachability mode. When people decide they must be right and that they don't need help, that mindset closes the road to growth. When you open your mind to growth, you realize there is a flood of resources available to you.

BRIAN KING

"I'M NOT THE PROBLEM"

"While the other kids were watching sports, I was pretending to be a superhero or writing poetry," Brian King explains. Brian struggled to connect with his peers. He "got lost in his imagination," and his peers didn't share his interests, leaving him feeling alienated and riddled with anxiety. Besides, he was accused of having attitude problems, being too self-critical, and not trying hard enough in school. The various doctors his parents consulted couldn't identify the cause of his problems, but he was diagnosed with depression and prescribed medication. No one understood his transition difficulties, his hypersensitivity to stimuli, or how confusing and overwhelming the classroom and playground environments were for him.

But in grade school he found relief in the presence of a few caring teachers. For example, his art teacher noticed that Brian struggled with the classroom environment and making friends. "I would freeze," Brian explains. "I'd get overwhelmed. The room was so busy. I would sit there like a deer in headlights and wouldn't know what to do." His teacher would sit next to him, and, in a calming voice, explain the next step and give him the extra attention he needed. She met Brian at his current skill and functioning level, matched his pace, and never pushed him to figure things out on his own or work harder to catch up with everyone else. "When I felt isolated, alone, like no one saw me, she always saw me. I always felt safe with her."

That was okay, she never tried to shove me into a box and that has always been instrumental in how I've become. You can be the best teacher in the school and work wonderful with a kid on the spectrum, but you are working with a child who has extreme trust issues because your predecessors blew it. So now you're competing with this child's baggage. And you know that you are basically starting from scratch and you have to somehow let this child know it's going to be different with you.

"Just meet the child where they're at, just take into consideration their history, what their story is and how you are a new character in the story, and you've got to earn your way in. It's not entitled to you."

Another crucial support was his grade-school English teacher, who appreciated his writing. Every assignment Brian turned in to her was gold. "She took the time to help me feel as though I was creating something of value. It was worth something to her to be able to read what I had written." This special attention pushed Brian to experiment more with his writing, which also became embraced by others, to such an extent that, in his words, "Writing has become a major aspect of how I engage with life experiences, life processes, and the way I now serve other people."

When Brian was diagnosed with autism as an adult, it liberated him and helped him understand how to best serve his three sons, who are also on the spectrum. "Up until then, I thought it was just me not being good enough," he admits. In Strategies for Building Successful Relationships With People on the Autism Spectrum: Let's Relate! (2011), Brian describes the revelation that came with his diagnosis: "I realized the problem did not lie with me. The problem lay with the lack of a fit between me and the rest of the world. The problem was that disconnect. The problem wasn't me, and the problem wasn't anybody else. It was that we didn't know how to bridge that gap between us" (p. 37).

"I believed that here was something wrong with me, and all the feedback was that you need to try harder. You need to put forth more effort, you need to be more motivated. Oh yeah, nobody could put their finger on it ... it was piecemeal, you know? Oh he's depressed, let's take a pill. Oh he's got generalized anxiety, let's give him a pill for that. Or he's just shy, he's too self-critical. Again, it was all on me."

"My autism was seen as behavior; it was my attitude. There were other things like that: I was overly sensitive, I was too emotional, I was too dramatic. People didn't realize the transition issues and the hypersensitivity and all of the sensory challenges I had; how confusing and overwhelming the classroom was, and the playground situation was intolerable."

"It was all oversimplified as simply an attitude problem."

COMMUNICATION BREAKDOWN

In his professional life, Brian has worked as a relationship coach and has authored several books about navigating the social world and learning how to communicate in ways that build successful relationships for individuals both on and off the spectrum. Brian emphasizes that it is important for anyone working with an autistic individual to understand the basics of communication and acknowledge the multitude of different ways it can occur. This ultimately helps address communication problems parents may experience with their children. Due to the importance of communication and Brian's close personal and professional knowledge about the challenges inherent in this topic, I asked Brian to elaborate, as presented below.

What Is Communication?

Brian asks parents to reconceptualize how they look at communication, adapt their efforts, and redefine their expectations to connect with their children. "The discipline of communication focuses on how people use messages to generate meanings within and across various contexts, cultures, channels, and media" ("What Is Communication?" n.d., para. 1). More simply put, communication refers to the act of expressing oneself. We use many different forms of communication. For example, communication can consist of words, sounds, gestures, signs, or other behaviors. Some nonverbal autistics use voice augmentation devices, communication apps, and picture boards. Sometimes spoken words are not enough to communicate effectively. For example, imagine you are sitting in a booth at a crowded, noisy restaurant, and you recognize a friend at the entrance. You call the person's name, but your friend doesn't hear you. Next, you stand up, raise your hand, and wave your friend over to your table. The International Society for Augmentative and Alternative Communications (ISAAC; n.d.) identifies these supportive communicative behaviors as augmentative and alternative communication (AAC). Everyone uses this evidence-based practice (referred to as technology-based treatment/technology aided instruction and intervention by Wong et al. [2015]); it is the degree to which people use it that dictates their accommodation needs.

Communication problems. If a communication breakdown occurs, this means a message transmitted from sender to receiver wasn't understood. Brian emphasizes that this does not necessarily mean the sender was a poor communicator, nor that the intended receiver was a poor listener. It simply means the message failed. You wouldn't say a deaf woman using sign language wasn't communicating well if a verbal person who didn't know sign language couldn't understand her. Therefore, to enable communication, Brian says it is the responsibility of all involved parties to acknowledge (to the best of their abilities) the communicative needs of the others and attempt to adapt and connect.

Filling communication and socialization gaps. Both verbal and nonverbal autistics communicate – some communicate in ways familiar to mainstream society, whereas others have their own unique rules that must be discovered and shared for effective communication to take place. Autistic people who are verbal are able to articulate their communication or socialization difficulties to a verbally dominant society and receive help. But nonverbal autistics' modes of communication are not widely understood, and, as a result, it is easy to assume they have a problem and need therapy or more education to learn to speak "properly."

Brian suggests the most effective way to communicate with people on the spectrum is to adapt one's own ways of communicating to meet autistic individuals where they can be reached. This means making efforts to communicate with people of all abilities, even those who push us out of our comfort zone. Regular conversation with others reminds us we are all a part of the human race with similar desires and the ability to motivate, care for, and support each other throughout our lives.

Beyond verbal speech, Brian explains, there are also specific communicative and social behaviors that various societies value as useful or simply polite, such as eye contact or still bodies (no fidgeting). But these social behaviors, which come naturally to some (or are relatively simple for them to learn), are often especially difficult for autistics. One of these social behaviors is eye contact. Effective socialization occurs when people feel they are seen and heard; that they matter to the people they are communicating with. This can happen without eye contact. For example, people can listen intently with only fleeting eye contact, and demonstrate interest instead by nodding their heads, periodically asking questions, or summarizing what others are saying. Conversely, people can use eye contact and never truly engage with the person they are socializing with or understand what they are saying. Therefore, the emphasis on social behaviors such as eye contact may not serve a purpose beyond teaching a person how to appear more NT.

Brian wants parents to understand that if their child is unable or uncomfortable exhibiting communicative or social behaviors expected by others in conversation, they need to be sensitive to that. Because Brian is aware that social situations fatigue him, he has developed ways to advocate for himself to maximize his social options. For example, he prefers to socialize in quiet areas in low lighting. He also prefers to go to a restaurant either late in the morning or late in the afternoon when it is less crowded and there is little background noise. If he visits a friend's house, he sometimes asks to turn off a few lights to make it more relaxing for him. Brian's sons are also sensitive to noise. If they go somewhere as a family and know it will be loud, they bring headphones to drown out the noise around them and text each other to communicate. "People think we are ignoring each other, but we are in fact connecting in a very sensory-friendly way." Brian suggests everyone should take ownership of their skills and responsibilities in order to communicate effectively. Communication involves the capabilities and needs of two or more parties, and blaming others for the breakdown only delays the message transmission and belittles those involved.

EXAMINING YOUR AGENDA FOR YOUR CHILD

Parents who learn their autistic children's communication preferences can more easily meet their most basic needs and help them develop into confident, successful adults. In Brian's career as a life coach, he emphasizes the importance of raising people to reach their maximum potential. But he is quick to add, "Education comes in different forms. I'm not a big fan of the therapy mindset. It begins with the premise that something about you is wrong or insufficient." Instead, he suggests parents or relatives of children on the spectrum first make sure they are helping facilitate the child's agenda and not their own. "A lot of parents make the mistake of looking at themselves as the standard for what the real world looks like, and they try and steer their kids along that path, and their kid is likely nothing like them, and they're taking a very unique path."

> *"The people who force eye contact are an example of people using themselves as a standard."*

Some skills and behaviors are necessary for independent living, but there are a lot of ways to be independently successful. Brian encourages parents to help their autistic children discover their talents and then offer them an eclectic sample of successful living so they can see interesting and manageable paths to their goals.

Those who want to help autistics must be honest about whose agenda they are supporting. If at all possible, parents or other family should try to identify what their autistic children want help with. If the child does not have the knowledge and skills necessary to do this, families can help begin the search. Brian concludes, "The thought of my [autistic] kids going into the world unprepared fuels me. I want them to be valued instead of pitied by society."

"You need to learn to partner with other people who have the skill set you do not."

Autistic people may need or want help with anything from daily functional tasks to more complex professional ones. For example, people who live on their own and hold jobs need to know how to wake up on time, prepare meals for themselves, and navigate traffic. If these are skills autistic people have difficulty with, they can learn to seek out the help of someone who possesses that knowledge and find daily support. This may translate to reliable friends calling each morning to make sure they are awake, or asking others to deliver groceries or help prepare meals. Other supportive people might offer reminders about oil changes, or help make sure important bills are paid on time. Brian admits, "My life right now is a direct result of being helped. I am an interdependent human being."

REFLECTION QUESTIONS

▶▶ What is the most frustrating part of communicating with your child? What can you change in your communication style to reduce the frustration?

▶▶ When/where does your child have the greatest difficulty communicating with you (time of day, environments, etc.)?

▶▶ What do you see as your child's primary communication challenge? What does your child think is frustrating about the way you communicate with him?

▶▶ What future plans does your child have? What future plans do you have for your child? Compare answers.

▶▶ What challenges or obstacles do you see standing in the way of your child living as an independent adult? How might you encourage your child to find and receive these specific supports from people other than you?

The Empathy Myth and Educational Advocacy

AN INTERVIEW WITH SHAWNA HINKLE

"

There is nothing wrong with needing accommodations. It is okay to do things differently and to assert yourself and to say that you need something different." - Shawna Hinkle

SHAWNA HINKLE  "

ON THE OUTSIDE

"I knew there was something different. I knew there was something odd." Hinkle remembers feeling this way as she grew up in a small town that didn't have a lot of opportunities for social connections for her.

" I was always trying to figure out how to fix my differences." When she felt like an outsider, she studied the moves of her peers so she could imitate them exactly in the belief that, "If I copy how they act, then they will like me." She had peers she called "friends," but they weren't very nice to her.

"A lot of autistic girls I know socially try to blend in .. but there's just little things that later on you'll remember and [realize]... oh ... they were tricking me or you have a feeling that something isn't right."

Although she never felt she completely fit in, this feeling of separateness became her social norm, and she continued to pursue "friendships" with lowered expectations about how she should be treated. The girls weren't very nice to her. And although she didn't really understand at the time, she was seriously bullied.

While peer acceptance was very limited, Shawna had some positive experiences with teachers:

> I had two teachers that I liked. My second grade teacher- I don't really know exactly why-she was just really a nice teacher; she always included me. And I had a teacher when I was in ninth grade who really encouraged my writing and individualized assignments for me. I remember one time we were reading Shakespeare and the project was to put on a little play. Obviously I'm quiet and a little shy. She intuitively knew that, and she picked me and one of my friends to do a crossword puzzle as our project. I knew that she had done that so I wouldn't feel uncomfortable.

The pressure and anxiety of school and the lack of services led Shawna to quit school. "I quit school as soon as I could and ... I went and got my GED ... and I went to college. But I didn't last very long because I didn't have the skills to do it and didn't have the support."

> *"Had I known that I had Aspergers, then I would have been able to get the support that I needed."*

Later in life, after both of her sons were diagnosed with autism, Shawna began reading more about autism and was eventually diagnosed herself at the age of 31. As a result, she now understands more about the difficulties she experienced growing up. She realizes that she doesn't need loads of friends to be happy and is okay being alone at times. Shawna currently spends most of her time caring for her two young sons and advocating for their needs. She blogs regularly about her experiences and autism expertise, including empathy and educational advocacy.

THE EMPATHY MYTH

Shawna is one of many people on the spectrum who has written on the topic of empathy, attempting to inform the NT world that she, as well as other autistics, do have the ability to experience and react to the emotions of others. But because autistic people do not always react in ways others expect, they are sometimes labeled as callous, uncaring, obtuse, or oblivious.

Shawna gets overwhelmed by strong emotional experiences, and she'd rather deal with them privately. She is embarrassed about being upset and may not cry at the first word of a tragedy, but this doesn't mean she doesn't show empathy and isn't deeply moved by emotional events.

She explains that sharing emotions is a social event. Because she processes most social situations on an intellectual rather than an intuitive scale, she often shuts down when trying to process a shared emotion. However, Shawna asserts that even though she may feel overwhelmed and be unable to express her emotions typically, she still has the capability to care deeply for other people and experience the full range of human emotion. Shawna also sees this empathic spirit in her two autistic sons.

Shawna explains that her difficulty expressing emotion like NTs can also cause difficulty in her marriage because she and her husband both struggle to interpret each other's emotions. They have to verbalize everything they are thinking and feeling: when they're upset, why they're upset, and how the other can help fix the problem. They can't assume the other can figure out what they are thinking or feeling. But Shawna insists that this struggle doesn't signal an inability to empathize, but rather, a challenge in interpreting the ways emotions are expressed between them.

Shawna's assessment of her experience supports the theory of Swiss neuroscientists Henry and Kamila Markram, who propose that the fundamental problem autistic people experience is not related to a social deficiency, but instead to a "hypersensitivity to experience," which includes an overwhelming response to fear, emotions, and sensory input. The Markrams' theory suggests that individuals on the spectrum may actually experience more empathy than their NT counterparts, which can lead to different reactions to emotional events and misunderstandings of an autistic person's feelings or emotional and empathetic capacity (Alleyne, 2008).

If a person under-reacts to an emotional event, others may assume that he or she doesn't care as much or doesn't truly understand the emotional complexity of the situation. Unfortunately, autistic individuals have been judged in this way for years. They are often stereotyped as living "in their own world" with little regard for the rest of society. But withdrawal is a typical response to an overload of emotion or information. Shawna explains that while many autistics cope with emotional events in different ways, it doesn't mean their experience is less human.

As Cynthia Kim, author of the Musings of an Aspie blog, notes in her post "The Empathy Conundrum," it isn't as simple as deciding whether people on the spectrum possess empathy or not. She claims to have an "empathy deficiency." Kim explains, "I struggle with taking the view of another person spontaneously and instinctively." She asserts that this deficit does not mean she is unsympathetic, unemotional, or any less human. Rather, it means she may need more information than what is typical to understand a social situation. Some may find her reactions to emotional situations unconventional. In some situations, she may need to work harder to understand what comes instinctively to most people. But that's it, "Nothing more, nothing less" (Kim, 2013, "Choose Your Words," para. 16).

The Origin of the Empathy Myth

The idea that people on the spectrum lack empathy relates to a commonly-cited belief introduced by researchers Baron-Cohen, Leslie, and Frith (1985), whereby autistic individuals are thought to have "mind-blindness" or difficulty employing "theory of mind," the ability to imagine another person's thoughts and feelings. Empathy is often divided into two types. *Cognitive* empathy refers to the ability to interpret what another person is thinking or feeling whereas *affective* empathy refers to the sharing of another person's emotions (Carter, 2013). Some people on the spectrum struggle with cognitive empathy. Others may have difficulty with cognitive empathy in select situations or environments; however, this doesn't mean they lack all cognitive empathy skills, and it doesn't mean they don't possess affective empathy. Suggesting that autistic people lack empathy implies that they lack an important characteristic of humanity. This attitude can open the door to destructive power differentials between both parents and their children, and society and individuals on the spectrum. Sadly, this power differential can cause parents to be more dismissive of their children, and, in extreme cases, lead to physical and emotional abuse (Carter, 2013).

EDUCATIONAL ADVOCACY

Creating an IEP. Another area in which Shawna advocates for individuals on the spectrum (especially those of her two sons) is in school. The two main difficulties Shawna encountered with her sons' former school were creating IEPs that accurately reflected their needs and ensuring the teachers and administration implemented it. "My milder son didn't get enough support. They told him to 'suck it up and move on.' They also didn't have high enough expectations for my more severe son. For him, I had to make sure it [school] was not like daycare all day."

Students are eligible for an IEP if they have a disability that impacts learning or requires specialized instruction to progress at the same rate as their peers in a general education classroom, if they attend a public school. Shawna notes that although these lengthy packets of accommodations may appear permanent, parents still have every right to add or change elements to these plans at any time. The plan is formed based on data collected during several rounds of educational testing; however, the testing data only measure one particular moment of time, and parents can speak up if they think the results do not accurately represent their children. Further, the recommendations may not cover all of the specific needs of each child; they are educated guesses at what someone might need in an educational setting. Some of these include cognitive, fine-motor, gross-motor, speech, hearing, and vision needs.

It is important for parents to exercise the right to see their child's IEP several days before an IEP conference so they have time to review the plan and come prepared to discuss the recommendations and any suggestions they have for revisions.

Shawna adds that one of the most important issues she sees with parents advocating for their children in an IEP meeting is that they think the school staff members are "bigger players" in the IEP process. She reminds parents that they are equal members in the IEP formation team. "It sounds silly, but I have to keep repeating in my mind that I am just as good, knowledgeable, and valuable as anyone else at this table during a meeting."

Checking in. Shawna knows some parents feel more comfortable with their child's academic environment if they are given regular opportunities to check in with their children or teachers in this setting. She recommends that parents observe or participate in the classroom as much as they can to learn about their child's daily experience. If the school permits, parents of younger children can volunteer to help out in their children's classes so they can see their children executing the school routine. They could also set up formal observations. Instead of (or in addition to) observations, parents could ask special education aides to send daily communication sheets home where they have recorded any highs or lows for the day as well as any other specific information the parents have determined is important.

> *"My older son is in a general education classroom. His more 'mild autism' and people not really understanding has made it a million times worse. My other son has the opposite problem; he's nonverbal. He's so severe that they don't have high expectations for him."*

Shawna had the unfortunate experience of having to deal with her son coming home from school with unexplained bruises. Shawna was disappointed with how the school handled the situation. School officials were defensive from the start. "Instead of having my son's well-being at the forefront of the situation, they seemed to be much more concerned with trying to be sure to not implicate themselves in any wrongdoing." They couldn't explain her son's injuries, and she felt like they were afraid to address the situation, which made a resolution impossible. She explains that if the school's administrators had been respectful instead of hostile, more could have been done to resolve the situation. "They acted as if I were the enemy because I wanted to know what happened to my son."

Because the school did not offer the information or support she needed, she withdrew her son and decided to homeschool him. This underscores the importance of finding professionals you can trust and maintaining regular communication with them in order to ensure your child's academic, emotional, and physical safety.

REFLECTION QUESTIONS

▶▶ In what ways does your child show empathy?

▶▶ How can you revise your child's IEP or 504 plan to address social or emotional issues that may interfere with education?

▶▶ Have you and your child discussed your child's IEP? How can you encourage your child to be an active participant in the meetings?

▶▶ How do you know your child is safe, comfortable, and productive at school?

▶▶ In what ways have you established yourself as a competent advocate for your child in the school?

▶▶ How can you improve your communication with your child's school?

Chapter Eleven

Succeeding in the Workplace
AN INTERVIEW WITH GAVIN BOLLARD

Don't be afraid to be unusual because the skills that unusual people have are often highly sought.

GAVIN BOLLARD

WORKING TOO HARD

"My problem started when I realized that I wasn't able to get all my work done at work despite starting earlier and finishing later than all my colleagues," Gavin Bollard, an Australian on the spectrum, explains. He had hurt his hand on the job due to overuse and his low muscle tone, which Gavin says is a high-risk problem for people on the autism spectrum because their lifestyles and body makeup increase the chance and severity of these issues. For example, his low muscle tone and hyperflexibility, coupled with a hyperfocus and a computer-centered job, resulted in him engaging in work all day without even realizing he was in pain. His job load had recently increased, and he wasn't aware his body couldn't keep up.

"It didn't occur to me that I needed to talk to my boss about the problem. I simply felt that I wasn't putting enough time into it. It was only when a colleague saw my swollen arms and hands and realized how much pain they were in that they told management and got an intervention sorted out for me."

His workplace relied heavily on his skills, and his boss supported several interventions to help him regain the physical stamina necessary to perform. For example, his boss found someone to type for him during his healing period and saw to it that his workspace was rearranged, including the installation of dictation software. His company also supported acupuncture therapy, which Gavin found helpful in reducing the sharpest pains. They also sent him to a gym with a personal trainer to work on rebuilding the muscles needed for his job. Gavin also installed software that would help him break through his hyper-focused concentration periods and alert him whenever he spent more than an hour at the keyboard. These supports, along with the help of a colleague who would check in throughout the day and ensure Gavin took breaks, helped him manage his pain and regain productivity.

His condition returned a few times, but never as severe as the first. Since this experience, Gavin learned to detect early signs and manage the symptoms. He also learned to self-advocate and tell his boss when a project needed more resources. "One of my common phrases when a large new project is given high priority is 'okay, which ball do you want me to drop in order to get this done?'" This verbal reminder encourages a discussion of his current workload and priorities so some of his less critical work can be reallocated to a junior employee.

Gavin never felt "normal" in a job, and, once he was diagnosed at 37, this unease made more sense.

"I don't think that it [ASD diagnosis] means a great deal though. To me, it just means that I'm a little different in my actions, motivations, capabilities etc. I can still feel comfortable around 'normal' people – except when emotions run high."

SUCCEEDING IN THE WORKPLACE:
Preparation, Finding The Ideal Environment, And Mentorship

Once autistic people enter adulthood and obtain meaningful work, they still face obstacles to success. Gavin learned to navigate the work world with several accommodations for his social difficulties. For example, he didn't apply for a job unless he fulfilled 90% of the criteria. It was important for him to realize his personal and professional needs, and he made professional choices that supported them.

"Accept yourself and BE yourself. Don't be afraid to be unusual because the skills that unusual people have are often highly sought. Be aware of your own needs, such as the need for space and solitude and make sure that your employment choices support these. Also, follow your special interests. You'll want to be employed for a long time, so make sure that you pick an area that YOU personally enjoy."

Autistic people can have difficulty finding, maintaining, or climbing the ranks in a job for a variety of reasons. Gavin says he is successful in his professional life because he has worked with the same company for 15 years, he is paid well, and he enjoys his work. But he admits his autism has interfered with his ability to climb the corporate ladder. At one point, he had a higher position, but found it too difficult to manage other people and maintain upper-management connections, so he changed jobs and says, "I'm glad I don't have that position any more."

Employers' First Impressions

Too many people on the spectrum are only given surface assessments, quick judgments based on how they look or move in a small frame of time. A 2015 study illustrates the challenges ASD individuals face with job interviews and consequent struggles to gain employment. The study's authors audio-recorded employment conversations with 20 adults on the spectrum (who tested in the average range for problem-solving and nonverbal IQ) and with 20 who did not have autism. The audio-recordings were played back for 59 university students who were asked to rate communication quality on a second-by-second basis. The students noted significantly more deficits in speech, grammar, vocabulary, speed, and social behaviors in the autistic individuals. The study concluded that the listeners would offer only 30% of the autistic group a second interview, compared with 75% of the nonautistic group (Mitchell & Roux, 2015).

Preparation. "Work needs to start at home," says Gavin. All parents have the difficult task of preparing their children for the complex social, physical, and mental demands of the work environment. When your children are young, you can begin by expecting them to contribute to the household by performing regular chores. Gavin suggests that, when possible, try to motivate them by explaining that chores help the family or help mom and dad, rather than constantly rewarding them with sticker charts or other external motivators. Gavin admits that some kids respond well to reward charts, but he tries not to do this with his two sons on the spectrum. When they help out, sometimes he will reward them with extra computer time, a later bedtime, or a special dessert, but he doesn't constantly remind them of these rewards as motivation to help out around the house.

Sometimes Gavin's children need the individual steps of a chore broken down for them to be able to complete it successfully. He believes this is important to teach them skills needed in the workplace:

Chores need to be done properly. My father had a saying: "If it's worth doing, it's worth doing well." I never really understood how important that was until I watched my own kids take the garbage out by dragging the bag through the house and down the driveway (where it burst on the cement and all the contents spilled out). These days my wife and I say to our kids, "Take the garbage out by carrying, not dragging the bag. Make sure that all of the rubbish goes into the bin outside, make sure that it is all pushed down below the top of the bin and that the lid is closed afterwards." Even then, some mornings I still get up and find rubbish strewn all over the driveway or into the neighbor's yard – and I have to pick it all up before I go to work. We've discovered that if we constantly reiterate all of the steps and checks, that it eventually (and that's the key word, "eventually") sinks in and becomes second nature. We're worried that employers won't take the time to break down all of the steps or go through proper "quality assurance" with our kids, so it's important that they know to do everything to the best of their ability.

Gavin suggests that if parents ensure that everyone in the family contributes to the work necessary to run the household, and if they model and foster the correct behaviors for completing chores, their children are more likely to carry responsible behavior through to the workplace.

Finding the ideal work environment. Gavin suggests that, as with any child, it is best to encourage children on the spectrum to explore professions within their particular skill sets or areas of interest. While some autistic individuals work better in areas that allow them to focus on independent tasks and avoid social settings, it is a mistake to assume this is the route for everyone. Gavin adds that some job screening is necessary because not all employers are willing to make accommodations for new employees that they might make for senior employees. Gavin comments, "If your child has a sensitivity to fluorescent lights, for example, perhaps an office job is not the best starting point."

The Value of Autistic Employees

Each person on the spectrum has different skills to offer the job marketplace, and many employers (like Gavin's) understand their value. In 2013 The Financial Times published an article about a father from Denmark who quit his job as a chief technology officer to start Specialisterne, a company that recruits autistic people to work on data entry, software programming, and testing projects (Jacobs, 2013). Other companies share this recruitment strategy. The software company SAP also acknowledges the special skills of many autistic adults and has even established a goal to have at least 1% of its workforce made up of people on the spectrum by 2020 (McGraw,

2014). While some may argue that recruiting autistics is a form of reverse discrimination, it still stands that only those candidates capable of performing and excelling at the desired skill sets would be considered for employment. The targeting of autistic people for employment is a new attempt to recognize the value they have to contribute to the workplace as well as society at large. There is no one particular job environment that works best for all autistic people; however, autistic individuals can still benefit from some general tips to help establish a foundation for professional success. In an article in Human Resource Executive, Marcia Scheiner, president of the Asperger Syndrome Training and Employment Partnership said that most autistic individuals are more likely to thrive when they have a specific understanding of what they are expected to deliver. In addition, most work best in an environment with clear communication with job tasks and expectations clearly defined (McGraw, 2014). Scheiner says a company's human resources (HR) department should lead the way to making workplace accommodations for autistic people and offering themselves as an accessible resource.

Finding a mentor. Gavin also sought out workplace mentors whom he could rely upon for support, hints, and corrections. As a result, he has learned that if he is nudged or "spoken-over" by one of these trusted coworkers, it is a signal to stop whatever he is doing. He also has coworkers who check in with him to make sure he is taking breaks so he doesn't exhaust his body by working too intensely. According to Gavin, the best neurotypical people to work with are those who are mentors.

He believes finding a mentor can help people establish work-related goals as well as receive support during a potentially rocky transition to a new position. As mentors get to know new workers, they can also help advocate for their coworkers' needs and help set them up in the best working environment to enhance productivity and overall employee satisfaction. HR can be a good resource for discovering who an appropriate mentor might be and facilitating the initial conversation about mentorship.

After Gavin found a good professional niche, he could begin building relationships with his coworkers. Gavin has been successful working for 15 years as the IT head for a regulatory banking body that utilizes both his special interest in computing and his technical skills. He has found a good professional fit, and his coworkers have recognized his talents.

"People at work now rely upon my abilities and perception, such as being able to remember product keys and serial numbers, being able to recall large chunks of computer code, IP addresses and word-for-word conversations. A few years ago, they would have been 'weirded out' by it." Gavin says his professional success is a result of his ability to "see the big picture and think logically." For example, many of his IT troubleshooting methods involve him assessing situations by "looking" from the point of view of the code. This was another ability that used to weird out his colleagues, but is now accepted as a valuable technique.

REFLECTION QUESTIONS

▶▶ What specific obstacles does your child face in becoming a productive member of the workforce?

▶▶ How can you encourage your child to pursue jobs you believe are appropriate fits?

▶▶ What difficulties does your adult child have in meeting job demands?

▶▶ How can your child learn to self-advocate at work?

Chapter Twelve

Pushing Your Child's Limits
AN INTERVIEW WITH ANGELA ANDREWS

> *Autism is not a disease; it is an integral part of my personality. To 'cure' my autism is to 'cure' who I am. There are many people in this world with personality traits I cannot stand; however, I do not attempt to 'cure' them.*
>
> ANGELA ANDREWS

A DIFFERENT PATH

"Her thinking is different than anything I've ever seen before," Angela Andrews' kindergarten teacher announced to Angela's mother, and then went on to explain that Angela had given strange answers to some of the questions on her intelligence test – a test administered to all students before they entered first grade. To further clarify, the teacher gave Angela's mother the following example. Each child was shown a picture of a barn; inside was a farmer milking a cow surrounded by several other animals. The image covered about 90% of the paper, and most children taking the test spoke about what was going on inside of the barn. However, Angela spent the entire time talking about how it was dark and raining outside of the barn. Her description was accurate, but not typical. The teacher told Angela's mother to watch her development because she was taking a different path than other children.

Angela did develop differently, which allowed her a valuable perspective in raising her two autistic children. Angela insists that even though people on the spectrum develop differently and experience different obstacles to development, they still have to learn how to survive in mainstream society. She has first-hand experience working through the difficulties of growing up autistic in a society that doesn't adequately understand and accommodate for autism, and she is now helping her children do the same.

DON'T SHELTER YOUR CHILD

Parents act with the best intentions: They want to protect their children from ridicule; they want to see their children succeed; or they just want them to be happy. However, Angela cautions that parents who shelter their children deny them a full view of the world and, consequently, miss out on learning and growth opportunities. Autistic children tend to have difficult childhoods due to their socialization differences, and their parents sometimes want to protect them in such a way that it interferes with their ability to thrive independently in an NT society. Lydia Wayman discusses the importance of having balanced relationships because it exposes people to a larger representation of society than if they would only spend time around other autistics or strictly NTs.

Angela underscores the importance of forcing societal integration so autistics can learn to develop in an NT society. "If you shelter an autistic, cater to their negative symptoms, and keep them apart in a false environment, you are writing a recipe for their failure." While it's important to acknowledge opportunities to make accommodations for autistics, it is nevertheless critical to help them learn to cope in mainstream society.

Gradual exposure. Angela used gradual exposure to help her autistic son gain greater access to the NT world. "They [autistic children] cannot have the world exactly as they wish, so they must learn to cope." Angela recognized her son's environmental fears (particularly ceiling fans and large stores) and approached them by adopting an exposure therapy strategy which addresses phobias in a safe environment and retrains the brain to no longer recognize the fears as threats. Angela encouraged gradual, consistent exposure to his phobia while providing a safe place to retreat if necessary. Her teenage son had many phobias over the years, some developing suddenly. She had difficulty discerning a cause, so it was important to have a plan to help him safely address each one so they didn't overwhelm him and limit his access to society.

One of her son's fears was ceiling fans. At first, Angela would keep a ceiling fan on for a few minutes at a time in their house while her son was playing a video game, an activity he enjoyed. She then gradually increased the duration, careful not to trigger a meltdown because she was trying to teach him other ways to communicate his stress and didn't want to reinforce tantrum behavior. Once they were visiting a friend who had a sunroom with a fan on because of the extreme heat, and Angela didn't let her son demand the fan be turned off. Instead, he avoided the room for a while until he was comfortable approaching and then joined the group later. Now her son has learned to control his thoughts and feelings in situations where he sees a ceiling fan.

This [control] will lead to his ability to integrate himself into the world with far more success than if I demanded every restaurant, store, or home with a fan shut them off because he was uncomfortable. Discomfort is what pushes us to grow and to change. You don't try to change what isn't bothering you. You only try to change what causes you unease. This is what every neurotypical child must do and so must every autistic child. The difference in this, which parents need to be taught, is how it is approached.

Angela also used this strategy over a period of about two years to teach her son how to enter large shopping buildings.

First, he was in the back of the cart with a blanket over it and ear muffs on. Then, we removed the earmuffs. Then we wrapped him in the blanket, but he could see out. Then we let him hold the blanket in the cart. Then he walked next to the cart holding the blanket. Now I wish to God that child would stay anywhere near the darn cart so I can get out of the grocery store in some normal amount of time! However, I am very proud he is where he is, annoying as it can be.

Angela has gently encouraged her children to have social experiences she believes will benefit them. The approach is crucial to whether or not a well-intentioned lesson results in healthy growth or a regression. The fact that a discomfort exists is not the problem. She supports their path to change by leading them in small steps and with constant love.

Social narratives for change. Another way Angela helped her children cope with environmental phobias and social anxieties was to use social narratives. There are many social narratives available online for parents to use, but Angela found it more effective to create her own that were customized to the specific situations her children encountered. She found social narratives to be especially helpful in preparing her autistic children to encounter people of authority who didn't understand or respect their challenges and needs. Angela created several stories about police officers because when her son became overwhelmed, he lost the ability to speak, and she worried this could be misinterpreted as defiance and lead to a stressful showdown with police. She also created social narratives about her children's disabilities and what they could do to circumvent them in specific situations. For example, she used one to teach her son to retreat to a safe, quiet room when he becomes overwhelmed at school. Not everyone will accommodate all the time, and, just like for all children, you have to "push their boundaries or they'll never grow."

DON'T LET THE DOOMSDAY PROPHETS HAVE THE LAST WORD

No one knows what the future will hold for your child. There will be plenty of people with low expectations for your child, just like there were (and are) for Angela herself. Angela has encountered people who don't understand autism and make bad assumptions about her:

> They assume I'm stupid or slow. They assume I cannot survive on my own. They assume I am aggressive or violent. They assume I am unable to have friends or relationships. They assume I cannot raise children appropriately. They assume I am asexual. They assume I am not worthy of their time or effort to get to know because I am "flawed."

When Angela's son was diagnosed, she worried the world would think the same about him. "When my son was originally diagnosed, I was terrified. It was like a death sentence for the child I thought I had given birth to." At the time, her son's doctors didn't give her much hope to think otherwise. But she began reading and researching on her own and seeing stories of hope, survival, and change. Although she had been told by her son's doctor that many therapies, including speech therapy, wouldn't be very helpful for her son, she read contradictory reports on her own and decided to try several activities despite the doctors' pessimistic predictions. Angela enrolled her son in ST, PT, OT, equine therapy, music therapy, and aqua therapy, all of which she found useful. Her son has made significant progress and is continuing to learn how to navigate mainstream society.

You may encounter doctors, psychologists, therapists, teachers, relatives, friends, or strangers who all have negative assumptions about your child's development or future capabilities, but it's your job to stay positive and offer support. This is important both because medical professionals are never right 100% of the time, and your child needs you to think positively about all human dignity and potential. Amid the negativity, people on the spectrum need a good support system to stay optimistic about their futures.

For Angela, her husband offered the support and understanding she needed to maintain a positive outlook and succeed both personally and professionally. Autistic individuals must know who they are and what they need as well as having someone standing behind them to support them along the way.

Angela points out that although autistic children may never speak, attend a general education class, or achieve scholastically, there is always a chance they will do these things and there are plenty of stories to prove the naysayers wrong. This was the case with Angela's son. Even though doctors predicted a horrible future for him, he wasn't listening. "The right supports, the right therapy, lots of love, and tons of patience are why he is where he is now. His future is bright, just like my elder, neurotypical son's."

The Benefits of Thinking Positively

The trite advice "think positively" may fuel more positive change than you think. The Huffington Post published an article discussing research on positive thinking conducted by Barbara Frederickson, a positive psychology researcher at the University of North Carolina (Clear, 2013). Frederickson conducted a study confirming how the brain shuts down to negative emotions such as fear or anger and comes to life when experiencing more positive emotions. In her study, she divided subjects into five groups and showed them a series of film clips. Groups 1 and 2 viewed clips with images of joy and contentment. Group 3 viewed clips with neutral images that didn't elicit any particular emotion. Groups 4 and 5 saw clips with images of fear and anger. The subjects were then asked to write what they would do if they were in a similar situation to that which they had just viewed. The groups that saw negative images wrote the fewest responses, while the groups that viewed positive images wrote considerably more, even more than the neutral group. It follows that when someone is feeling joyful or content, they see more possibilities in life. Frederickson believes regular positive thinking can develop a long-term ability to build skills necessary to lead a successful life, much like physical exercise improves a person's overall health. On the other hand, negative thinking can have the opposite impact (Clear, 2013).

Parents can also teach this attitude of positive growth to their children. Stanford psychologist Carol Dwek (2007) wrote about the benefits of a growth mindset. This concept is valuable for parents of children with disabilities (as well as typically developing children) to help them maximize their life potential and grow into confident, productive adults. Dwek's book explains that many people have one of two life perceptions: a fixed mindset or a growth mindset.

▶▶ Individuals with a fixed mindset believe their intelligence, talents or skills are fixed. In other words, they were born with a particular set of skills or a predisposition to develop certain talents (Dwek, 2007). This view can be extremely limiting. People with fixed mindsets assume their intelligence will lead to success. They also assume they cannot compete in many areas of life because they were not born with the skills to succeed like their counterparts were. Think of the benchwarmer on the basketball team who complains he wasn't born with the talent of his teammates. Or how often have you heard someone referred to as a "born leader," "born athlete," "born writer," or "born to play music," etc.? This perspective is common in our culture, but the idea that someone has a fixed intelligence and skills tends to limit growth.

▶▶ Those with a growth mindset believe they are capable of achieving more with the proper amount of work (Dwek, 2007). They understand that people have varying levels of skills, but they don't see every skill set as stagnant and then cozy up to a particular place in the human order. They believe brain power and talent are only a starting point to achieving more. They spend time developing intelligence and skills because they believe growth is possible with effort.

REFLECTION QUESTIONS

▶▶ What have you said (or thought) your child will never do?

▶▶ What specific obstacles prevent you from taking your child out in public?

▶▶ How can you arrange more successful public outings for your child?

Chapter Thirteen

Themes That Emerged From Interviews

As I reviewed the interviews generously granted to me by the 12 autistic adults, I noticed that certain topics resonated with many of them. These topics have been compiled as themes along with quotes from the interviewees.

BULLYING

Almost all of the autistic adults described experiences of being bullied as a child or young adult. The bullying came in many forms - they were called names, excluded and rejected, or physically harmed. They explained that the experience of being bullied continues to impact them into adulthood. Bullying creates deep wounds. Many of the interviewees also reported that during their school years their teachers either "turned a blind eye" when they were bullied or -- even worse -- participated in or led the bullying that they experienced.

▶▶ "Maybe we're the favorite target." Alyssa Hillary

▶▶ "Maybe the bullies are getting bolder ... as our teachers turn a blind eye." Alyssa Hillary

▶▶ "I was an outcast." Ben Kartje

▶▶ "The instances [of bullying] ... have stuck with me most of my life." Ben Kartje

▶▶ "I was never invited to anything." Ben Kartje

▶▶ "You're hurt a lot when you're an autistic kid, you ... wanted company desperately and it was just very tough ... to get on with people." Tim Page

▶▶ "[Some teachers] were real out and out bullies." Tim Page

▶▶ "I did feel utterly humiliated ... I was very aware of how different I was from the other kids." Jodie Van de Wetering

▶▶ "It may take me the rest of my life to build myself back up. I truly don't know why my friend ditched me, even now." Lydia Wayman

▶▶ "There's just little things that later on you'll remember. You have a feeling that something wasn't right." Shawna Hinkle

DIAGNOSIS

Prior to a diagnosis, many of the autistics asked themselves, "What is wrong with me?" Without understanding that autism was impacting behavior, those around them concluded that these children had bad attitudes or were just "bad kids." After years of being blamed for willful misconduct, the diagnosis of autism was often welcomed. The interviewees described the diagnosis as "liberating," "a relief," and "validating." A number of the adults wished that the diagnosis had come earlier. They believe that they would have gotten supports that would have changed their lives if only they had known about their autism sooner.

BEFORE THE DIAGNOSIS

▸▸ "Until then I thought it was just me not being good." Brian King

▸▸ "Why can't my brain process interactions like other people?" Kathy Gray

▸▸ "What's wrong with me, why can't I see things the way they do?" Amy Gravino

▸▸ "I never ever felt 'normal.'" Gavin Bollard

▸▸ "I'd known there was something 'wrong' with me for a long, long time." Jodie Van de Wetering

▸▸ "They basically wrote me off as a 'bad kid.'" Tim Page

▸▸ "It was all oversimplified ... as simply an attitude problem." Brian King

RESPONSE TO DIAGNOSIS

▸▸ "Actually [the diagnosis] was quite a liberation for my family entirely." Brian King

▸▸ "It was definitely really liberating for me." Shawna Hinkle

▸▸ "Well that explains a lot, that's the missing piece of who I am." Kathy Gray

▸▸ "About time." Alyssa Hillary

▸▸ "Diagnosis is a key to help kids and parents." Brian King

▸▸ "My own first emotion was incredible relief." Jodie Van de Wetering

▸▸ "I felt a great deal of relief, and quite validated." Lydia Wayman

▸▸ "Wow, this really does sound like me." Tim Page

LOOKING BACK ON THE DIAGNOSIS

▸▸ "Had I known ... I would have been able to get the support that I needed." Shawna Hinkle

▸▸ "I do blame the lack of awareness of what autism really looks like for the difficulties I had before my diagnosis." Lydia Wayman

▶▶ "I can't help but think that, had we had a name for [autism] ...things might have been different." Lydia Wayman

▶▶ "Had I been diagnosed younger, I could have had the same success throughout my scholastic career." Angela Andrews

▶▶ "It just means that I'm a little different in my actions, motivations, capabilities, etc." Gavin Bollard

▶▶ "Autism has made me who I am today." Ben Kartje

▶▶ "I don't talk about my formal diagnosis ... [because] it will be used in some way to delegitimize me." Lydia Brown

▶▶ "It's not who I am, but it's a part of who I am. I wouldn't be me without it." Amy Gravino

EDUCATION AND THERAPY

Relationships matter. Most of those interviewed expressed that effective teaching or therapy begins with feeling understood, accepted, and treated with respect. Opportunities to work with a mentor or to have a co-worker who takes on a mentorship role were also recommended by multiple respondents. Rules and routines matter. Many of the adults reported that explicit rules and structure are critical to their success. Participation matters. Autistic adults value the opportunity to contribute to decisions about goals and strategies selected for intervention. When that is denied, interventions are less meaningful and less effective.

GOOD TEACHERS

▶▶ "He was never mean about the issues I really did have." Alyssa Hillary

▶▶ "Tried her best to understand what I was going through day in and day out." Brian King

▶▶ "My teacher from year nine encouraged me to be my nerdy self." Gavin Bollard

▶▶ "She understood that there was something different about me, and catered to my strengths as well as weaknesses." Jodie Van de Wetering

▶▶ "She brings light wherever she goes." Lydia Wayman

▶▶ "Some adored me and treated me with incredible kindness." Tim Page

▶▶ "She met me right where I was at, and I always felt safe with her." Brian King

▶▶ "I looked back at how she believed in me." Brian King

▶▶ "She built my confidence." Angela Andrews

HELPFUL INTERVENTIONS

▸▸ "It is very helpful to have rules to understand where you fit." Tim Page

▸▸ "Therapy needs to be tailored to the specific needs of the individual." Jodie van de Wetering

▸▸ "Any work experience, even volunteer experience, is better than none at all." Gavin Bollard

▸▸ "I've come up with a system ... It is over and above what an NT person would need." Jodie Van de Wetering

▸▸ "The social skills stuff is much easier when the sensory sensitivities are under control." Jodie Van de Wetering

▸▸ "Mentorship is absolutely crucial." Lydia Wayman

▸▸ "Read Emily Post." Tim Page

▸▸ "Put the curriculum around the child instead of making the child fit into the curriculum." Shawna Hinkle

▸▸ "I need to understand the back plan or the theory behind everything." Lydia Brown

▸▸ "Get a job in high school; I learned a lot of good soft skills [there]." Kathy Gray

▸▸ "Helping us learn skills that we're capable of learning, helping us figure out how to work with the abilities we have, helping us find ways to communicate that work for us." Alyssa

▸▸ "It's nice when the instructors are explicit." Kathy Gray

▸▸ "Give people therapies for what they want, what would help them function in society." Ben Kartje

UNHELPFUL INTERVENTIONS

▸▸ "The people who force eye contact are an example of people using themselves as a standard." Brian King

▸▸ "We were all in high school, college, or about to go to college, and she is talking to us as though we're 5." Lydia Brown

▸▸ "Using cognitive behavior therapy (CBT) to analyze a situation that's already happened is far too late to change my emotions, opinions or reactions to what went down, and the whole process is frankly far too complicated for me to remember and apply in real-time during stuff that's happening now." Jodie Van de Wetering

▸▸ "My behavioral support specialist ... was so shallow and fake, and she viewed my autism as a defect that needed a remedy." Lydia Wayman

MASKING

Hiding, masking, camouflaging, pretending, acting - all words that describe a strategy used by some individuals with autism to help them to blend in with the neurotypical world. Nine of the twelve people interviewed for this book described using this strategy. Some saw masking as a necessary skill and others described it as exhausting. Autistics often feel required to look as neurotypical as possible in order to hold a job or to participate in the community.

▶▶ "Hiding sucked. One of the few things I ever tried to hide ... was the flapping, since my classmates in third grade kept calling me r*** over it." Alyssa Hillary

▶▶ "If you pretend to be someone you are not, you are going to put on a mask. You are not going to like the ending." Brian King

▶▶ "If you didn't know how much effort I was putting into [blending in ...], you wouldn't know there was an issue for me." Brian King

▶▶ "You're trying to act as NT as possible [to get a job]." Kathy Gray

▶▶ "A lot of autistic girls I know socially try to blend in." Shawna Hinkle

▶▶ "I would imitate exactly what [my peers] did." Amy Gravino

▶▶ "I've gotten to be extremely good at playing the public." Tim Page

▶▶ "I can 'pretend' very well on the surface, thanks to the social skills training." Angela Andrews

PARENTS' REACTIONS TO THE AUTISM DIAGNOSIS

Not every person interviewed described how each of their parents reacted upon learning that their child had been diagnosed with autism. For the ones who did, an interesting pattern appeared to emerge. The autistic adults described their mothers as diving in, doing research, and providing support. In contrast, those who described their father's reactions described them as criticizing, and distancing themselves. No broad conclusions can be drawn from this small sample, but it gives us something important to think about. More people are learning that they have autism everyday. How can we help families - whole families - to work together upon learning this news?

MOTHERS' REACTIONS

▶▶ "My mother's reaction was, 'Oh, I guess this is actually a thing, and this ... isn't normal? But the whole family does that.'" Alyssa Hillary

▶▶ "My mother's been very positive about it." Jodie Van de Wetering

▶▶ "My mom was very hesitant and questioned the validity of the diagnosis. She spent months just researching before she realized how pervasive autism really was in my life." Lydia Wayman

▶▶ "My mother dove in head first. She joined support groups. She found every book." Amy Gravino

FATHERS' REACTIONS

▶▶ "My father thought that labeling yourself is weak." Alyssa Hillary

▶▶ "My dad chose, and continues to choose, to ignore it." Lydia Wayman

▶▶ "My father, ... hearing those words and finding out about this, ... he kind of cut off." Amy Gravino

Chapter Fourteen

Advice From 12 Autistic Adults

This section covers additional advice to parents as well as information for autistic adults. Statements in this section are not direct quotes. Rather they are paraphrased statements because suggestions came from more than one of the autistic people who contributed to this book.

ADVICE TO PARENTS

▸▸ As always, the special interest is the biggest key to obtaining successful employment. If it is at all possible for your child to work in a field which somehow touches upon their special interest, then do whatever it takes to get there.

▸▸ Be aware of the strengths, needs, and differences of your child. Make sure that their needs are meant -- whether it is plenty of "alone-time," wait time, or a written list.

▸▸ Visual is generally the strongest way to help autistic people learn. Present information in writing or drawing, whenever possible.

▸▸ Therapy needs to be tailored to the specific needs of the individual.

▸▸ Tell your child that he has autism. All adults found that knowing their diagnosis of autism was important to their self-esteem and self-acceptance.

▸▸ Everyone's autism is different. Help your child to understand what his autism looks like and what it means to his life.

▸▸ Build autism into everyday conversation, as appropriate. Let your child know that nothing is "wrong" with him.

▸▸ Teach your child to advocate for her needs. Include advocacy as an IEP objective.

▸▸ Bullying by other students is rampant in schools. Address bullying in your child's IEP. Ensure that your child is protected.

▸▸ Request that teachers receive training about the impact of educational bullying on kids, and request administrators implement a no tolerance policy for teachers who bully students.

▶▶ Provide explicit instructions. "Clean up your room" does not have meaning by itself.

▶▶ Break down "cleaning" into parts that the child can do such as, "Put the clothes on the floor in the hamper," and "Stand all books up on the bookshelf." Think about putting these in a checklist.

▶▶ Prepare your child in advance of activities and teach your child to prepare herself.

▶▶ Teach and practice the rules for home and school.

▶▶ Ensure that your child has work experience when she is in high school. The autistic child who has a job in high school is more likely to get a job as an adult. This even applies to adults who are college bound.

▶▶ Make sure that everyone in the child's environment understands his sensory needs and how to address them. For many children, this step is necessary to start the learning process.

▶▶ Tell your child when he is doing something right.

▶▶ Make sure that your child learns conversation skills. Conversation skills are the best predictor of employment, independent living, and having meaningful relationships.

▶▶ A safe environment at home and school is essential. Autistic children and adolescents should feel safe in the halls, in the lunchroom, in class, etc …

▶▶ Autistic students should not be encouraged to act neurotypical; they should be encouraged to match their behavior to their environment to the extent that they can.

▶▶ Help your child to develop mentors throughout his life.

▶▶ Teach skills that lead to life success. Many of these skills are not strictly academic, such as:

- Developing and following a budget

- Paying bills without a reminder

- Learning how to solve problems

- Having a conversation -- verbally or nonverbally -- with others, including calling a plumber, when needed, or talking with a potential landlord.

ADVICE TO AUTISTICS

▸▸ Be aware of your own needs, such as the need for space and solitude and make sure that your employment choices support these.

▸▸ Understand your autism --the gifts it brings and the challenges it presents.

▸▸ Follow your special interests. You'll want to be employed for a long time, so make sure that you pick an area that YOU personally enjoy.

▸▸ Learning how to interact with others is important. Social skills classes that are targeted to your needs and strengths can be helpful.

▸▸ If you have a problem or concern, the wait-and-see method is often not the best solution.

▸▸ Consider reading popular self-help books, such as "How To Win Friends And Influence People" or an etiquette book. A lot of people read these -- not just autistic people.

▸▸ Look for a mentor -- someone you can ask questions of and emulate. Your relationship needs to be very open and honest.

▸▸ Be an advocate for yourself.

▸▸ If you do not understand something, ask a friend or trusted adult.

▸▸ Partner with other people who have the skill set you do not.

▸▸ You are not broken -- you are wonderful. Sure, you have to learn some skills and perhaps you will need to do some things differently. Almost everyone does.

▸▸ Although everyone blends in sometimes, know that you are meant to be who you are.

Chapter Fifteen

Teaching Self-Advocacy: Advice From the Autistic Community

Many of the themes that emerged from these interviews challenge parents and caregivers to be better advocates for their children, teenagers, and adults on the spectrum.

Most parents are interested in autism advocacy because they want to help their autistic children successfully navigate this world and enable them to get the support and tools they need to maximize their quality of life. To achieve these ends, parents must both understand how to best advocate for their children and how to teach them to self-advocate. The 12 interviewees are advocates for themselves and others like them. More specifically, their advice related to education, therapy, and autism interventions will hopefully help families like yours learn advocacy skills necessary to achieve levels of confidence, independence, and happiness for the autistic individuals in your life. This section expands upon these self-advocacy themes addressed in the interviews and explores ways to teach self-advocacy skills with advice based on the opinions and expertise of Lydia Brown and other adults on the autism spectrum.

When autistic children are young, their parents and families are their best advocates. But autism self-advocacy is crucial for achieving varying levels of independence and improving confidence. Parents may grow comfortable advocating for their children, navigating the educational world of IEPs and 504 plans, making appropriate sensory accommodations, and seeking patient, caring friendship opportunities, but, when possible, this knowledge and skill must eventually be transferred to autistic children.

Teaching autism self-advocacy skills offers many crucial benefits:

▶▶ It builds the self-confidence and fulfillment needed to learn, work, and live productively (Shore, 2006).

▶▶ It helps achieve varying levels of independence as children learn to communicate their specific needs and utilize their talents (Shore, 2006).

▶▶ It promotes peace and acceptance, teaching society to embrace disability and improve living for all autistic or other people with disabilities.

What Exactly Am I Teaching My Child?

Below are some suggestions for teaching children on the spectrum how to self-advocate.

- Teach them about autism – It is important for people on the spectrum to know what autism is in order to understand exactly how they are affected by it. Autism is a complex neurological condition, but children can learn some of the basic diagnostic criteria, and parents can encourage them to read the writings of other self-advocates who describe autistic living. Autism affects individuals in different ways, but it is helpful if they at least understand how they are affected and how this plays out in their daily lives (Shore, 2006).

- Teach them how to articulate their strengths and weaknesses – Honest, personal assessment of strengths and weaknesses is difficult for both autistics and neurotypicals alike. Parents can start by asking their children to try and identify their strengths and weaknesses and then provide additional examples and illustrate how they impact their lives on a daily or long-term basis. Parents can stress that everyone has strengths and weaknesses and that the more self-aware you are, the greater opportunity you have for growth (Shore, 2006).

- Practice when to disclose their needs – Help your child learn that self-advocacy is important, but there is a time and a place for full disclosure. Parents can teach the child to request their needs, but not to over-share. They can offer examples of situations where it might be appropriate to request a specific accommodation and when the children can either delay or achieve a preference on their own (Williams, 2014).

- Practice how to disclose their autism – Parents can teach their children about safe people to disclose their specific needs to. This may include teachers, disability advocates, or employers, depending on the child's particular situation. Parents can help their children practice saying a statement that explains their most important needs, such as particular sensory sensitivities. They may also help them type a statement about their educational needs that they could give to new teachers (Williams, 2014).

- Teach them to find and utilize appropriate resources – A critical skill to autism self-advocacy is knowing how to continually find resources to meet your needs. This means finding the right people to express your needs to. Parents can tell their children about specific advocacy and disability support organizations that have a broader understanding about disability policy and resources on local, state, and national levels. A list of these organizations may be found in the resource section at the end of Chapter One.

Learning and teaching how to advocate for your child's needs is essential to helping your child lead an independent and productive life. Teaching and modeling how to live a positive, meaningful autistic life will help you and your child embrace what you cannot control and truly appreciate your child's identity.

ADVOCACY IN COLLEGE

To be independent, autistic individuals must develop adult living skills, like managing a bank account, doing laundry, and maintaining an orderly living space. While attending college, they must also learn specific job skills, meet new academic demands, all while managing their emotions and developing a healthy new routine. Lynne Soraya, author of the "Asperger's Diary" for Psychology Today spoke of her struggles adjusting to college in an article for the Child Mind Institute. "Life skills like learning how to effectively manage sensory inputs so that you can safely cross a street are still applicable for those of us deemed 'high functioning,'" Soraya explained (Arky, "The challenges of independence," 2014, para. 1).

When she was in college, Soraya was hit by a car. On the day of the accident, she had gotten into an argument that emotionally overwhelmed her, creating tunnel vision that, when accompanied by the outside noise and crowds, blinded her from noticing the car until it was too late. Soraya's story illustrates the physical dangers autistic individuals can potentially face on a daily basis. Parents can help their autistic children learn how to cope with these different social, emotional, and academic situations they will encounter in college (Arky, 2014).

Tips for Helping Autistic Students Survive and Thrive in College

The Autistic Self Advocacy Network (ASAN) acknowledges the need for support during the transition to college in an eBook Navigating College, which offers advice from several current and former college students on the spectrum. ASAN recommends a variety of ways people on the spectrum can prepare for the various demands of their new lives before launch time. The ability to self-advocate will help your child continue to thrive. Some recommendations from ASAN are:

> ▶▶ **Explore available support** – Even though the law requires accommodations be made for students with disabilities, it doesn't clarify how this applies to college students. Many colleges have prioritized special education supports and offer programs designed to help disabled students on the spectrum succeed (Carlotti, 2014). For example, Mercyhurst University in Erie, Pennsylvania, offers special services for

individuals with AS or ASD. Through the help of a graduate mentor, the program offers optional meal gatherings, AS support groups, and special trips to both on- and off-campus events. Other schools, like Rutgers University, prefer to completely mainstream autistic students, but still offer a variety of individual support services through their College Support Program for Students on the Autism Spectrum (Kapp, 2013). Regardless of the chosen college, if there are specific resources available to help people on the spectrum, it will be important for your child to know the contact information of the most relevant people who can address his or her needs (Kapp, 2013).

▶▶ **Request a single dorm room** – A single dorm room relieves an autistic student from dealing with the complex social negotiations required between people living in close quarters. Lydia Brown (2013) wrote about this issue, pointing out that sharing a dorm room is a social situation not discussed in most social skills classes. Lydia explained that these situations are more complex and intricate than determining whether a relationship with another person is friendly or trustworthy, or potentially harmful or disadvantageous. You are forced to interact with this person on many levels, and for the Autistic person, that can be overwhelming, daunting, and exceedingly difficult, especially if the roommate happens to be a neurotypical. (p. 60)

A single room will not further isolate, but rather offer autistic students the privacy and comfort of home and give them the confidence and energy to pursue successful social experiences of their own choosing.

▶▶ **Teach a respect for social boundaries** – Your child will be entering into a new social realm without constant adult supervision. Remind your child of appropriate social behaviors (both how to respect the boundaries of others and how to protect their own). Teach your child about how to identify sexual harassment and establish safe social behaviors (Sinclair, 2013).

▶▶ **Help your child practice self-advocacy** – There is a lot you can do to help set your child up for college success, but you can't control everything. Parents can teach their children to advocate for their special needs and not quietly suffer. Having a documented diagnosis will help autistic students acquire specific services, but also help them with the obstacles they might encounter on a daily basis. For example, parents can have their children practice what they might say to a peer or professor about their disabilities and their particular learning needs (Davis, 2013).

▶▶ **Help your child establish a daily organization plan** – Assist your child in creating visual calendars to help maintain organization. If waking up to an alarm is an issue, then encourage your child to have multiple alarms set each night. You can also help your child establish a study schedule during free time and use timers to signal when to switch subjects if necessary. Some students find it helpful to switch study locations after a certain period of time to help them transition their focus. Encourage your child to find a place to study that doesn't trigger any sensory sensitivity. You can assist with some of this planning before school begins, but it will be impossible to know every issue until your child begins executing a daily schedule. You can also encourage your child to maintain a healthy, organized schedule the same way Alex Eveleth does in his essay "Campus Living" from Navigating College (Ashkenzy & Latimer, 2013). He tells individuals on the spectrum, "Remember that maintenance of the essentials will help you keep going on academics – you won't be as effective in the library if you're missing sleep, meals, or showers" (p. 63).

▶▶ **Encourage relationships with professors** – Most college-aged students already know that establishing a relationship with a teacher can go a long way in determining their academic success. The same is true for college. Students may approach their teachers or professors with questions they have regarding content covered in class, additional help they might need preparing for a long-term assignment, or to share interesting news related to their coursework. In addition, special needs students may need to communicate any academic difficulties related to their disabilities. This is important so professors know how to alter their teaching to benefit more students (Davis, 2013).

▶▶ **Encourage them to join a club or activity** – Colleges are likely to have many more activities and organizations than were available in high school. This is a great opportunity for autistic students to find a social niche within their interest area. Participating in too many activities early on may overwhelm your child, but one club, organization, or extracurricular activity could be a way to have fun, relax, and meet new people (Davis, 2013).

▶▶ **Know your child's rights** – After high school, students are no longer covered by the mandates of the Individuals With Disabilities Education Act (IDEA), which requires a free and appropriate education be made available to all students regardless of disability, and supports the formation of IEPs. But the Americans With Disabilities Act (ADA) and Section 504 of the Rehabilitation Act of 1973 still offer protections for college students from discrimination based on disability (Sinclair, 2013). Colleges and universities must provide reasonable academic accommodations and modifications for students with disabilities in order to make the education system more equitable. Obtaining an accommodations letter from the college will help professors learn how to modify their class instruction to meet their students' needs. Most schools have disability support staff that will draft these accommodations letters for you (Sinclair, 2013). Jim Sinclair's introduction to the eBook Navigating College offers many additional legal tools for setting a solid foundation for academic success (Ashkezany & Latimer, 2013, pp. 7-28).

RESOURCES

- Welcome to the Autistic Community **(http://autisticadvocacy.org/2014/02/welcome-to-the-autistic-community/)** – ASAN offers guides for both adolescents and adults who are newly diagnosed. This resource answers some common questions about autism and autism self-advocacy and explains neurodiversity.

- Accessing Home and Community-Based Services: A Guide for Self-Advocates **(http://autisticadvocacy.org/home/projects/books/accessing-hcbs/)** – This guidebook offers information about community-based services, including Medicaid waivers and other government programs. It also teaches autistic people how to organize their own support service programs.

- Self-Advocacy Curriculum **(http://autisticadvocacy.org/wp-content/uploads/2015/02/CurriculumForSelfAdvocates_r7.pdf)** – According to ASAN, the self-advocacy curriculum is "a tool that is intended to help individuals with autism and other developmental disabilities learn more about the self-advocacy movement; celebrate neurodiversity; cultivate local self-advocacy groups; and ultimately, become and remain empowered through self-advocacy."

- "The Future (and the Past) of Autism Advocacy, Or Why the ASA's Magazine, The Advocate, Wouldn't Publish This" by Ari Ne'eman, former president of Autistic Self Advocacy Network – Ari Ne'eman offers advice on how interested parties can help advocate for people on the spectrum.

- The Don't Freak Out Guide to Parenting Kids With Asperger's by Sharon Fuentes and Neil McNerney – This book helps parents learn to handle challenges associated with raising children on the spectrum and appreciate their children in the process.

- Center for Parent Information and Resources **(http://www.parentcenterhub.org/ repository/idea/)** – This website offers well-organized information on everything you need to know about IDEA.

- "Building a Transition Plan" **(http://www.autismafter16.com/article/03-07-2012/ building-transition-plan)** – This article discusses the legal requirement of goal setting and implementation plans for students after high school who have IEPs.

- "Incredible Colleges for Students With Special Needs" **(http://www. bestcollegesonline.com/blog/2011/09/21/20-incredible-colleges-for-special-needs- students/)** – This resource published by Best Colleges Online includes a list of colleges.

- "Special College Programs for Students With Autism" **(http://www. bestcollegesonline.com/blog/2011/05/25/10-impressive-special-college-programs- for-students-with-autism/)** – This is another list published by Best Colleges Online.

- "Colleges With the BEST Learning Disability Programs" **(http://www.huffingtonpost. com/2010/06/07/best-ld-programs_n_603369.html)** –This is a list from Huffington Post of the best colleges for students with a learning disability.

- "Programs for Students With Asperger Syndrome" **(http://www. collegeautismspectrum.com/collegeprograms.html)** – This is another list of colleges with autism support programs.

- The Parent's Guide to College for Students on the Autism Spectrum by Jane Thierfeld Brown, Lorraine Wolf, Lisa King, and G. Ruth Bork – This book helps parents guide their autistic child through the college selection process, understand their child's legal rights, develop a supportive educational plan, and teach their child to become an independent self-advocate.

- Peterson's Colleges for Students With Learning Disabilities or AD/HD – This guide lists the services offered at over 900 different two- and four-year colleges in the United States and Canada.

- Navigating College by Ashkenazy & Latimer – This ebook published by the Autistic Self-Advocacy Network is written specifically for autistic students who are about to enter college; however, parents can benefit from reading it as well.

References

- About SPD. (n.d.). Retrieved July 17, 2018 from **http://www.spdfoundation.net/about-sensory-processing-disorder/.**

- Alleyne, R. (2008, September 17). Autism is caused by a 'supercharged' mind, scientists claim. The Telegraph. Retrieved July 18, 2017 from **http://www.telegraph.co.uk/news/health/2976839/Autism-is-caused-by-a-supercharged-mind-scientists-claim.html.**

- American Psychiatric Association. (2000). Diagnostic and statistical manual of mental disorders: DSM-IV-TR. Washington, DC: American Psychiatric Association.

- Autism Speaks. (n.d). FAQs: State autism insurance reform laws. (Retrieved March 2, 2018 from **https://www.autismspeaks.org/advocacy/insurance/faqs-state-autism-insurance-reform-laws.**

- Baron-Cohen, S., Leslie, A. M.. & Frith, U. (1985). Does the autistic child have a "theory of mind?" Cognition, 21, 37-46.

- Bascom, J. (Ed.). (2012). Loud hands: Autistic people speaking. Washington, DC: Autistic Self Advocacy Network.

- Bollard, G. (2015). What is "stimming" and why is it important? [Web log post] Retrieved January 17, 2017 from **http://special-ism.com/what-is-stimming-and-why-is-it-important/.**

- Brown, L. (2013). Autism and dorm life. In Autistic Self Advocacy Network. (Ed.), Navigating college: A handbook on self-advocacy written for autistic (pp. 59-62). Washington, D.C.: The Autistic Press.

- Brown, L. (2014, December 4). One of the most awesome people that ever happened to me [Web log post]. Retrieved June 15, 2018 from **http://www.autistichoya.com/2014/12/kitay-davidson.html.**

- Carter, L. K. (2013). Autism and empathy [Web log post]. The Huffington Post Blog. Retrieved from **http://www.huffingtonpost.com/liane-kupferberg-carter/autism-and-empathy_b_3281691.html.**

- Centers for Disease Control and Prevention (2018). Autism spectrum disorder: Data and statistics. Retrieved August 1, 2018 from **https://www.cdc.gov/ncbddd/autism/data.html.**

- Clear, J. (2013, July 10). The science of positive thinking. Huffington Post Health Living Blog [Web log post]. Retrieved July 18, 2018 from **http://www.huffingtonpost.com/james-clear/positive-thinking_b_3512202.html**

- Cognitive behavioral therapy and autism. (2015, November 23). Retrieved January 15, 2018 from **http://researchautism.net/interventions/15/cognitive-behavioural-therapy-(cbt)-and-autism.**

- Davis, S. A. (2013). Safety. In Autistic Self Advocacy Network. (Ed.), Navigating college: A handbook on self-advocacy written for autistic (pp. 89-90). Washington, D.C.: The Autistic Press.

- De Marino, A. (2013, August 29). Motor planning and organization. Retrieved March 2, 2018from **http://www.icare4autism.org/news/2013/08/motor-planning-and-organization/.**

- Dwek, C. (2006). Mindset: The new psychology of success. New York, NY: Ballantine Books.

- Evans, M. (2012). And straight on till morning. In J. Bascom (Ed.), Loud hands: Autistic people speaking (pp. 162-166). Washington, DC: Autistic Self Advocacy Network.

- Eveleth, A. (2013). Social issues. In Autistic Self Advocacy Network. (Ed.), Navigating

- college: A handbook on self-advocacy written for autistic (pp. 127-130). Washington, D.C.: The Autistic Press.

- Fierberg, R. (2016). Meditation as a potential treatment for autism spectrum disorder [Web log post]. Retrieved March 2, 2018 from **http://www.parents.com/blogs/parents-perspective/2013/11/22/the-parents-perspective/meditation-as-a-potential-treatment-for-autism-spectrum-disorder/.**

- Grandin, T., & Panek, R. (2014). The autistic brain: Helping different kinds of minds succeed. New York, NY: Houghton Mifflin Harcourt.

- Haupt, A. (2014, April 9). How to be a friend to someone with autism. U.S. News and World Report. Retrieved March 2, 2018 from **http://health.usnews.com/health-news/health-wellness/articles/2014/04/09/how-to-be-a-friend-to-someone-with-autism**

- Hilary, Alyssa (n.d.) Yes, that too. Retrieved June 1, 2018 from **http://yesthattoo.blogspot.com/search/label/Bullying.**

- International Society for Augmentative and Alternative Communication. (2015). Communication methods. (2015). Retrieved July 1, 2018 from **https://www.isaac-online.org/english/what-is-aac/what-is-communication/communication-methods/.**

- Jacobs, E. (2013, June 6). A father who saw untapped forces in his son's autism. Financial Times. Retrieved March 2, 2018 from http://www.ft.com/intl/cms/s/0/ ba2d5706-ccf5-11e2-9efe-00144feab7de.html - axzz3OYciMMgv.

- Kalmeyer, D. (2010). An introduction to applied behavior analysis. Retrieved from http://www.ctfeat.org/articles/Kalmeyer.htm

- Kapp, S. (2013). Higher education transitions. In Autistic Self Advocacy Network. (Ed.), Navigating college: A handbook on self-advocacy written for autistic (pp. 30-35). Washington, D.C.: The Autistic Press.

- Neurodivergent K. (2016). You, yes you, need autistic friends. Retrieved August 1, 2018 from https://30daysofautism.blog/2016/06/21/you-yes-you-need-autistic-friends/.

- Kim, C. (Jan 17, 2013). The empathy conundrum [Web log post]. Retrieved March 2, 2018 from http://musingsofanaspie.com/2013/01/17/the-empathy-conundrum/.

- King, B. (2011). Strategies for building successful relationships with people on the autism spectrum: Let's relate. London, England: Jessica Kingsley Publishers.

- Kutscher, M. L. (2014). Kids in the syndrome mix of ADHD, LD, autism spectrum, Tourette's, anxiety, and more! London, England: Jessica Kingsley Publishers.

- McEachin, J. J., Smith, T., & Lovaas, O. I. (1993). Long-term outcome for children with autism who received early intensive behavioral treatment. American Journal on Mental Retardation, 97(4), 359-372.

- McGraw, M. (2014, January 30). Setting up autistic employees to succeed. Human Resource Executive Online. Retrieved March 2, 2018 from http://www.hreonline.com/ HRE/view/story.jhtml?id=534356658.

- McPhilemy, C., & Dillenburger, K. (2013). Parents' experiences of applied behavior analysis (ABA)-based interventions for children diagnosed with autistic spectrum disorder. British Journal of Special Education, 40(40), 154-161.

- Minute movements of autistic children and their parents provide clue to severity of disorder. (2014, December 1). Retrieved March 2, 2018 from http://news.medicine. iu.edu/releases/2014/12/movements.shtml.

- Mitchell, W., & Roux, A. (2015). Life course outcomes research, A.J. Drexel Autism Institute, Philadelphia; May 13-16, 2015, International Meeting for Autism Research, Salt Lake City, Utah.

- Morin, A. (2014). Understanding executive functioning issues. Understood. Retrieved from **https://www.understood.org/en/learning-attention-issues/child-learning-disabilities/executive-functioning-issues/understanding-executive-functioning-issues.**

- The National Autistic Society. (n.d.). Sensory differences. Retrieved March 2, 2018 from **http://www.autism.org.uk/sensory.**

- Neurodivergent, K. (2014, May 28). You, yes you, need autistic friends. Retrieved from http://timetolisten.blogspot.com/2014/05/you-yes-you-need-autistic-friends.html

- Orenstein, B. (2014, March 5). This no-cost, drug-free therapy helps children with autism. Everyday Health. Retrieved March 2, 2018 from **http://www.everydayhealth.com/news/this-no-cost-drug-free-therapy-helps-children-with-autism/.**

- Page, T. (2007, August 20). Parallel play: A lifetime of restless isolation explained. The New Yorker. Retrieved August 1, 2018 from **https://www.newyorker.com/magazine/2007/08/20/parallel-play.**

- Page, T. (2009). Parallel play: Growing up with undiagnosed Asperger's. New York, NY: Anchor Books.

- Patino, E. (2014, April 7). Understanding dyspraxia. Retrieved March 2, 2018 from **https://www.understood.org/en/learning-attention-issues/child-learning-disabilities/dyspraxia/understanding-dyspraxia.**

- Peete, H. R. (2013, April 2). Autism, meet adolescence … Kaboom! One momma's perspective, fears and solutions [Web log post]. The Huffington Post Parents Blog. Retrieved March 2, 2018 from **http://www.huffingtonpost.com/holly-robinson-peete/autism-awareness-day_b_2991931.html.**

- Post, P., Post, A., Post, L., & Post Senning, D. (2011). Emily Post's etiquette (18thed.). New York, NY: William Morrow.

- Potterfield, J. (2013). Natural environment teaching. Retrieved March 2, 2018 from **https://sites.google.com/site/thebcbas/aba-toolbox/natural-environment-teaching.**

- Prizant, B. M., & Fields-Meyer, T. (2015). Uniquely human: A different way of seeing autism. New York, NY: Simon & Schuster.

- Sarris, M. (2013, July 23). Autism in the teen years: What to expect, how to help. Interactive Autism Network Simons Simplex Community. Retrieved March 2, 2018 from **http://www.iancommunity.org/cs/simons_simplex_community/autism_in_teens.**

- Schopler, E., & Mesibov, G. B. (Eds.). (2013). Learning and cognition in autism. New York, NY: Springer Science & Business Media.

- Sequeira, S., & Ahmed, M. (2012, June 4). Meditation as a potential therapy for autism: A review. Autism Research and Treatment. doi:10.1155/2012/835847.

- Shapiro, J. P. (1994). No pity: People with disabilities forging a new civil rights movement. New York, NY: Three Rivers Press.

- Shore, S. (2006). The Secrets of Self-Advocacy: How to Make Sure You Take Care of You. Autism Advocate, 44 (4). Retrieved February 11, 2019 from https://phxautism.org/wp-content/uploads/secrets-of-self-advocacy.pdf.

- Silberman, S. (2015). Neurotribes: The legacy of autism and the future of neurodiversity. New York, NY: Penguin Random House.

- Sinclair, J. (1992). Bridging the gaps: an inside-out view of autism (or, do you know what I don't know?). In E. Schopler & G. B. Mesibov (Eds.), High functioning individuals with autism (pp. 294-301). New York, NY: Springer Science+Business Media.

- Sinclair, J. (1993). Don't mourn for us. Our Voice, 1(3). Retrieved July 1, 2018 from **http://www.autreat.com/dont_mourn.html.**

- Sinclair, J. (2013). Introduction. In Autistic Self Advocacy Network. (Ed.), Navigating college: A handbook on self-advocacy written for autistic (pp. 7-28). Washington, D.C.: The Autistic Press.

- Stewart, R. (n.d.). Should we insist on eye contact with people who have autism spectrum disorders? Retrieved from **http://www.iidc.indiana.edu/pages/Should-We-Insist-on-Eye-Contact-with-People-who-have-Autism-Spectrum-Disorders.**

- Terra, C. (2012, May 26). The hidden autistics. Aspie Strategy. Retrieved July 1, 2018 from **http://www.aspiestrategy.com/2012/05/hidden-autistics-aspergers-in-adults.html.**

- Wang, K. (2012, April, 4). Autistic home decorating: Make your home autism friendly [Web log post]. Retrieved June 1, 2017 from http://www.friendshipcircle.org/

blog/2012/04/10/autistic-home-decorating-make-your-home-autism-friendly/.

- What is communication? (2015). Retrieved June 1, 2108 from **https://www.natcom.org/ discipline/.**

- Wilkins, S., & Burmeister, C. (2015). FLIPP the switch: Strengthen executive skills. Shawnee Mission, KS: AAPC Publishing.

- Williams, K., & Roberts, J. (2015). Understanding autism: The essential guide for parents. Wollombi, Australia: Exisle Publishing Ltd.

- Winslet, K., & Ericsdottir, M. (2012). The golden hat: Talking back to autism. New York, NY: Simon & Schuster.

- Winter, P. (2012). Loud hands & loud voices. In J. Bascom (Ed.), Loud hands: Autistic people speaking (pp. 115-128). Washington, DC: Autistic Self Advocacy Network.

- Wong, C., Odom, S. L., Hume, K. A., Cox, A. W., Fettig, A., Kucharczyk, S., ... & Schultz, T. R. (2015). Evidence-based practices for children, youth, and young adults with autism spectrum disorder: A comprehensive review. Journal of Autism and Developmental Disorders, 45(7), 1951-1966.

APPENDIX: TERMS AND CONCEPTS

Below is an explanation of a few terms used throughout this book.

Person-First vs. Identity-First Language

Some autism advocates prefer identity-first language over person-first language. In other words, they refer to individuals on the spectrum as autistic rather than people with autism. This choice is because the separation of personhood from autism suggests the autism is not a part of their identity, which some take issue with. They argue that the desire to separate their autism from their personhood suggests it is an affliction they can (and should) rid and still maintain their true personalities. Lydia Brown is one example of an advocate who prefers identity-first language and is not ashamed to be called autistic. Lydia explained that while many self-advocates use identity-first language, it's still important to determine the preference of the individual on the spectrum and respect it instead of assuming your personal decision about this issue is the most appropriate in every situation for all people.

Others prefer to use person-first language, referring to individuals on the spectrum as people with autism rather than autistic people. This choice represents the desire to emphasize their humanity or personhood before their autism. People I have spoken to who prefer this language have said that autism doesn't define them. They've said even though they live their lives with autism, that doesn't mean it always has to be the primary defining description.

For example, in an interview I conducted with Paul Isaacs, a British autism advocate, trainer, and public speaker, he said:

"With regards to my identity, I see myself as a part of humanity, so therefore I am a person first – personally, my autism affects my visual and auditory perception, language processing, cognitive processing, learning difficulties, etc., but these are part of me, not the totality of my being."

Neurotypical

Sometimes I use the term neurotypical (NT) to refer to a person who is not autistic. This is a label used in the autistic community for this purpose as well. This term could technically apply to anyone with an atypical neurology (including dyslexia, attention deficit hyperactivity disorder [ADHD], or bipolar disorder, for example). In this book, there are several instances when a contributor or I have used NT to signal a reference to someone who is not on the autism spectrum.

Neurodiversity

Neurodiversity is the concept that encourages the acceptance of a variety of different neurological conditions. It asks people to embrace neurological differences, treating everyone with dignity and respect. In general, this term can be applied to neurological differences such as ADHD, bipolar disorder, dyslexia, Tourette syndrome, and ASD, among others. For the purposes of this book, neurodiversity refers to the autism advocacy concept that treats autism as a neurological variation, or, "a different way of being human" (Prizant & Fields-Meyer, 2015, p. 4), rather than a disease or an illness.

Ableism

Ableism refers to discrimination against somebody based on a disability. It is a set of beliefs that identify people as socially or morally inferior based on their physical, emotional, developmental, or psychological disability. Ableism can be hidden in a person's subconscious. Lydia Brown speaks out frequently on how ableism can lead to the inferior treatment of autistic individuals and pressure them to hide or "cure" autism. All autism advocates have good intentions, but sometimes their approaches are offensive, as Lydia explains in Chapter One.

Medical vs. Social Model of Disability

The medical model of disability suggests a person's disability is a problem that lies within the individual. The social model of disability suggests that disability occurs when a person's environment is not suited to that individual. For example, the medical model of disability would assume autistic individuals are disabled if they can't concentrate in a classroom with fluorescent lights. The social model of disability would suggest the lights are the problem and that changing the lighting would eliminate the disability in this situation.

Gender-Neutral Pronouns

Two of this book's contributors prefer to be identified using gender-neutral pronouns. Both Lydia Brown and Alyssa Hillary identify with the gender pronouns they, them, and theirs, and sections describing them may use these pronouns. The use of gender-neutral pronouns respects gender preferences by not assuming gender identity.

ABOUT THE EDITOR-AUTHOR

JENNA GENSIC

Jenna Gensic is a freelance writer and disability advocate from northern Indiana. She has four children; her oldest is diagnosed with cerebral palsy and autism. Jenna has a BA in English and an MA in English writing; she taught high school English before making the decision to work from home and raise her young children. She manages the Learn from Autistics website (learnfromautistics.com), and writes and speaks about parenting issues related to prematurity, cerebral palsy, and autism.

ANGELA ANDREWS

Angela Andrews is a data architect and analyst and the mother of five. She graduated from St. Mary's College in Notre Dame, Indiana, where she studied child development, learning and cognition, social psychology, and psychological disorders. She also earned a master of science in data analysis from Southern New Hampshire University.

GAVIN BOLLARD

Gavin Bollard is an Australian autism blogger and information technology specialist for a regulatory banking body. He has two sons who are also on the spectrum. Gavin blogs about some of the positive aspects of autism at Life with Asperger's **(http://life-with-aspergers.blogspot.com/)** with the overall aim "to increase the amount of first-hand knowledge about Asperger's." His blog includes several series articles to help parents and children on the spectrum with a variety of topics, including autism acceptance, bullying, advocacy, medication, and employment.

LYDIA BROWN

Lydia X. Z. Brown is a gender/queer and transracially/transnationally adopted East-Asian autistic activist, writer, and speaker, whose work has largely focused on violence against multiply marginalized disabled people, especially institutionalization, incarceration, and policing. Lydia is co-president of TASH New England, chairperson of the Massachusetts Developmental Disabilities Council, and an executive board member of the Autism Women's Network. In collaboration with Elesia Ashkenazy and Morénike Giwa-Onaiwu, Lydia is the lead editor and visionary behind All the Weight of Our Dreams, the first-ever anthology of writings and artwork by autistic people of color. Lydia's work has been featured in various publications, including Criptiques, Torture in Healthcare Settings, Disability Intersections, Black Girl Dangerous, POOR Magazine, and The Washington Post.

AMY GRAVINO

Amy Gravino is an author, autism consultant, and public speaker. She also runs a private consulting business called A.S.C.O.T. (Asperger's Syndrome Coaching and Other Techniques). She is a certified college coach for individuals with AS and advocates for autistics through her work as the director of Public and Community Relations for the Global and Regional Asperger Syndrome Project (GRASP) and as a board member for the Daniel Jordan Fiddle Foundation. She speaks regularly about autism and sexuality and is currently writing a book, entitled The Naughty Autie: Not Your (Neuro)typical Dating Guide. More information about Amy's professional services may be found at **http://www.amygravino.com/.**

KATHY GRAY

Kathy Gray was born in Asia and adopted at the age of 2. She attended school in Colorado where she earned a BS in Human Development and Family Studies. Kathy has experience working in a variety of service settings, including hospitals, group homes for adults with developmental disabilities, home-based childcare, and preschool education. Kathy was married in August of 2014. She enjoys spending her weekends with her husband and stepson (pictured) and blogging.

ALYSSA HILLARY

Alyssa Hillary is a graduate student in mathematics. Alyssa studied math, mechanical engineering, and Chinese as an undergraduate. An autistic activist, Alyssa is a public speaker and a contributor to a variety of publications, including writing and designing the cover art for the essay anthologies Criptiques and Typed Words: Loud Voices. Alyssa studied in Tianjin, China and blogs at Yes, That, Too **(yesthattoo.blogspot.com).**

SHAWNA HINKLE

Shawna Hinkle is a writer, autism advocate, and stay-at-home mother of three disabled children (two of whom are on the autism spectrum). She is fierce educational advocate for her children and homeschool teacher of one of her autistic sons. She blogs at Inner Aspie **(http://inneraspie.blogspot. com/)** about her experiences parenting in an atypical household.

BEN KARTJE

Ben Kartje is a special events employee at the University of Notre Dame and an avid Irish fan. He has a Black Belt in Tae Kwon Do and enjoys playing the drums in his spare time. He is active in his church and plays the drums for a local youth group. His life motto is: Always be yourself. Do not become the personality that is convenient.

BRIAN KING

Brian R. King, LCSW (ADHD & ASD Life Coach), is a #1 best-selling author, 28-year cancer survivor, adult with dyslexia, ADHD, and Ehlers-Danlos Syndrome. He's also the father of three sons on the autism spectrum. He is known internationally for his books and highly engaging presentations that teach the power of connection and collaboration. His strategies empower others to overcome their differences so they can build powerful and lasting partnerships. His motto is: We're all in this together.

TIM PAGE

Tim Page is an author, producer, biographer, and professor of music and journalism at the University of Southern California. He was a culture writer and music critic for The New York Times, the chief music critic of Newsday, and he won the Pulitzer Prize for criticism in 1997 for his writings about music for The Washington Post. He is the author or editor of more than 20 books, including Dawn Powell: A Biography, The Glenn Gould Reader, The Unknown Sigrid Undset, Carnegie Hall Treasures, and Parallel Play, a memoir. As a child, Tim was the subject of the short film, A Day With Timmy Page. He lives in South Los Angeles.

JODIE VAN DE WETERING

Jodie van de Wetering is a writer, speaker, and stand-up comic based in Queensland, Australia. After a lifetime of being seen as weird and willfully difficult, she was diagnosed with Asperger Syndrome in her mid-20s. Since then she's been researching, learning from other people on the spectrum, and figuring out who she is all over again.

LYDIA WAYMAN

Lydia Wayman is an autistic writer, speaker, and advocate who encourages people to see greatness in others, not despite our differences but because of them. She began blogging at Autistic Speaks **(https://autisticspeaks.wordpress.com/)** in 2009 and has been featured in The Wall Street Journal and on Good Morning America. Lydia speaks at autism conferences and has published articles designed to educate others about the many facets of autism, including the unique challenges related to living with mitochondrial disease. She has also self-published a book inspired by her blog entitled Living in Technicolor: An Autistic's Thoughts on Raising a Child With Autism.

CPSIA information can be obtained
at www.ICGtesting.com
Printed in the USA
LVHW061448301219
642042LV00019B/1183/P